CAMBRIDGE LIBRARY COLLECTION

Books of enduring scholarly value

Archaeology

The discovery of material remains from the recent or the ancient past has always been a source of fascination, but the development of archaeology as an academic discipline which interpreted such finds is relatively recent. It was the work of Winckelmann at Pompeii in the 1760s which first revealed the potential of systematic excavation to scholars and the wider public. Pioneering figures of the nineteenth century such as Schliemann, Layard and Petrie transformed archaeology from a search for ancient artifacts, by means as crude as using gunpowder to break into a tomb, to a science which drew from a wide range of disciplines - ancient languages and literature, geology, chemistry, social history - to increase our understanding of human life and society in the remote past.

Records of the Reign of Tukulti-Ninib I, King of Assyria, about BC 1275

In the preface to this 1904 work by Leonard King (1869–1919) of the British Museum's department of Egyptian and Assyrian antiquities, he states that the text it presents 'is of great historical value, inasmuch as it supplements our knowledge of the history of Assyria and her relations with Babylonia during the early part of the thirteenth century B.C.'. The tablet containing the text was buried under the wall of a city founded by King Tukulti-Ninib I (transliterated as Tukulti-Ninurta by modern scholars), to commemorate its building and his previous military achievements, which included the invasion of Babylonia. This account confirms earlier documents, and gives more detail on the chronology of a crucial period in the ancient history of the Near East. The book offers a lengthy introduction on the tablet and on the tradition of such foundation documents, as well as the cuneiform text and a parallel translation, along with an appendix of related documents.

T0382123

Cambridge University Press has long been a pioneer in the reissuing of out-of-print titles from its own backlist, producing digital reprints of books that are still sought after by scholars and students but could not be reprinted economically using traditional technology. The Cambridge Library Collection extends this activity to a wider range of books which are still of importance to researchers and professionals, either for the source material they contain, or as landmarks in the history of their academic discipline.

Drawing from the world-renowned collections in the Cambridge University Library and other partner libraries, and guided by the advice of experts in each subject area, Cambridge University Press is using state-of-the-art scanning machines in its own Printing House to capture the content of each book selected for inclusion. The files are processed to give a consistently clear, crisp image, and the books finished to the high quality standard for which the Press is recognised around the world. The latest print-on-demand technology ensures that the books will remain available indefinitely, and that orders for single or multiple copies can quickly be supplied.

The Cambridge Library Collection brings back to life books of enduring scholarly value (including out-of-copyright works originally issued by other publishers) across a wide range of disciplines in the humanities and social sciences and in science and technology.

Records of the Reign of Tukulti-Ninib I, King of Assyria, about BC 1275

*Edited and Translated from a
Memorial Tablet in the British Museum*

Leonard William King

CAMBRIDGE
UNIVERSITY PRESS

CAMBRIDGE
UNIVERSITY PRESS

University Printing House, Cambridge, CB2 8BS, United Kingdom

Cambridge University Press is part of the University of Cambridge.

It furthers the University's mission by disseminating knowledge in the pursuit of
education, learning and research at the highest international levels of excellence.

www.cambridge.org
Information on this title: www.cambridge.org/9781108082419

© in this compilation Cambridge University Press 2019

This edition first published 1904
This digitally printed version 2019

ISBN 978-1-108-08241-9 Paperback

This book reproduces the text of the original edition. The content and language reflect
the beliefs, practices and terminology of their time, and have not been updated.

Cambridge University Press wishes to make clear that the book, unless originally published
by Cambridge, is not being republished by, in association or collaboration with,
or with the endorsement or approval of, the original publisher or its successors in title.

Studies in Eastern History.

I.

RECORDS OF THE REIGN OF TUKULTI-NINIB I, KING OF ASSYRIA, ABOUT B.C. 1275.

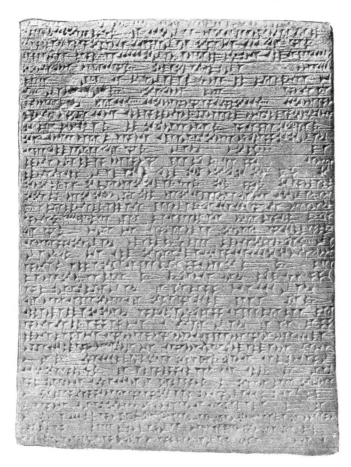

Limestone tablet inscribed with the Annals of Tukulti-Ninib I,
King of Assyria. [Brit. Mus. No. 98494, Obverse.]

Studies in Eastern History.

RECORDS

OF THE

REIGN OF TUKULTI-NINIB I,

KING OF ASSYRIA, ABOUT B.C. 1275.

EDITED AND TRANSLATED FROM A MEMORIAL TABLET
IN THE BRITISH MUSEUM

BY

L. W. KING, M.A., F.S.A.,

ASSISTANT IN THE DEPARTMENT OF EGYPTIAN AND ASSYRIAN ANTIQUITIES
IN THE BRITISH MUSEUM.

LONDON:
LUZAC AND Co.
1904.

HARRISON AND SONS,
PRINTERS IN ORDINARY TO HIS MAJESTY,
ST. MARTIN'S LANE, LONDON.

PREFACE.

———◆———

SOME two years ago, in the first volume of *The Annals of the Kings of Assyria*, issued by the Trustees of the British Museum, a collection was published of all the historical inscriptions of the early Assyrian kings, from about B.C. 2000 to B.C. 860, which are preserved in the British Museum. In that work the period between the reign of Adad-nirari I, about B.C. 1325, and that of Tiglath-pileser I, about B C. 1100, is represented only by a brick-inscription and some votive texts inscribed upon fragments of clay bowls. In fact, the only historical inscription of any length belonging to the early Assyrian period which had up to that time been recovered was the memorial tablet of Adad-nirari I, brought from Môṣul by the late Mr. George Smith in 1875. In the present volume the text is published of a very similar memorial tablet of Tukulti-Ninib I, the grandson of Adad-nirari I, which is of great historical value, inasmuch as it supplements our knowledge of the history of Assyria and her relations with Babylonia during the early part of the thirteenth century B.C.

The limestone tablet from which the text is taken was made by the orders of Tukulti-Ninib I, who had it

buried as a foundation memorial in, or under, the wall of
the city of Kar-Tukulti-Ninib, which was situated near
the Tigris between Kuyunjik and Ḳalʻa Sherḳât.   The
text contains an account of the founding of the city by
the king and the building of the city-wall, preceded by
a list of the military expeditions which he had conducted up to the time the tablet was engraved.   From
these records we learn for the first time of extensive
conquests to the north and east of Assyria made in a
series of expeditions by Tukulti-Ninib I, who closes the
narrative of his campaigns by an account of his invasion
of Babylonia and the complete subjugation of Sumer
and Akkad.

   That Tukulti-Ninib I conquered Babylon and ruled
it for seven years during the period of the Third, or
Kassite, Dynasty was already known from a tablet of
the "Babylonian Chronicle," and it has been suggested
that the Babylonian king he conquered was Bibe, or
Bibeiashu, whose name occurs in the Babylonian List
of Kings, and on a fragment of the "Synchronous
History" of Babylonia and Assyria, and upon some
votive objects found at Nippur.   From his memorial
tablet we learn that the opponent of Tukulti-Ninib was
Bibeiashu, who was not only defeated but was deported
to Assyria.   The new text thus confirms the suggested
synchronism between Babylonian and Assyrian history,
and is of great importance in its bearings upon the
problems of Babylonian chronology.

In addition to the publication of the new memorial
tablet, the texts and translations are given of a number
of supplementary inscriptions which treat of the history
and date of Tukulti-Ninib I. Of these mention may be
made of the portion of the "Babylonian Chronicle"
dealing with Tukulti-Ninib's reign, and the famous copy
of Tukulti-Ninib's seal-inscription written upon a tablet
of the time of Sennacherib, by means of which the date
of Tukulti-Ninib is fixed. In the account of the conquest of Babylon by Tukulti-Ninib on the former of
these two documents, I have succeeded in deciphering
the name of Bibeiashu, which has escaped the notice of
those who have hitherto edited and translated the text.
On the latter I believe I have made out the meaning of
the line of archaic characters, twice repeated on the
tablet, which has puzzled translators of the text during
the last thirty years. According to my interpretation
the line in question gives the name and title of
Shagarakti-Shuriash, the father of Bibeiashu, who is thus
proved to have owned the seal before Tukulti-Ninib
captured it in Babylon. Sennacherib's scribe was un-
familiar with the Old-Babylonian character in which
the name was written upon the seal, and he did not
recognize many of the signs, but he has made a fairly
accurate copy of their general form. On p. 69 I have
given a conjectural restoration of the original text, and
below it I have added the forms of the signs as they are
found upon Sennacherib's tablet. I think a glance at

this will suffice to show that the suggested interpretation is correct.

In the Introduction to this volume an analysis and description are given of Tukulti-Ninib's memorial tablet, and the information which it supplies on the early history of Assyria is fully treated. An attempt has also been made to discuss the class of foundation memorials to which it belongs, and a comparison has been drawn between the origin and object of these documents and those of the foundation deposits found during recent years under the walls and pavements of Egyptian buildings dating from the Fifth Dynasty down to the Ptolemaic period. It may here be added that the recent find of foundation-pits by Mr. Howard Carter at the entrance to the tomb of Ḥâtshepset at Dêr el-Baḥarî supports the theory as to the origin of the Egyptian foundation deposits which is suggested below. The object of the Babylonian and Assyrian foundation memorials was of a less magical and more practical character than that of the Egyptian foundation deposits. With the Babylonian practice we may fairly compare our custom of burying coins and current newspapers in the foundations of public buildings at the present day, though it is unlikely that the newspapers will serve our purpose as effectively as the stone and almost imperishable clay have preserved the records of the early kings of Western Asia.

As the text of the memorial tablet of Tukulti-Ninib I

is of great interest for the study of Assyrian epigraphy, the tablet is published in facsimile in a series of outline blocks. The text which accompanies the translation and transliteration is printed in the larger cuneiform type of Messrs. Harrison and Sons, which was specially designed from the lapidary forms of the later Assyrian characters.

The present book is the first in a series of small volumes which I have prepared on various epochs in the history of Western Asia. In addition to a number of historical studies the volumes will contain unpublished documents which throw new light upon the periods of which they treat.

My thanks are due to Dr. E. A. Wallis Budge for his help during the preparation of the work.

L. W. KING.

LONDON,
October 3rd, 1904.

CONTENTS.

———✦———

LIST OF ILLUSTRATIONS.

———◆———

INTRODUCTION.

THE materials for writing the history of Assyria, until the end of the twelfth century B.C., are very scanty, and any text which throws light upon the struggles and conquests of her earlier kings is of great value in determining the relations of the Northern kingdom with Babylonia, and in tracing the gradual rise of the former to a position of pre-eminence in Western Asia. A considerable portion of our knowledge of Assyrian history during this early period is obtained from two late documents, viz., the "Synchronous History," and a table inscribed with a section of the "Babylonian Chronicle"; both of these, when complete, contained brief summaries of the relations which existed between Assyria and Babylonia from the earliest times. Additional information concerning the campaigns and building operations of the early Assyrian kings is furnished by the historical inscriptions of later rulers, especially those of Tiglath-pileser I and Sennacherib. The contemporary records of the early kings themselves are our third principal source of information;

b

these comprise a few brick inscriptions and a number
of fragmentary votive texts inscribed upon clay bowls
with the object of recording the restoration of certain
temples of the gods.[1]

The only early Assyrian inscription of any length
that has hitherto been published is the famous memorial slab of Adad-nirari I, which was acquired for
the Trustees of the British Museum at Môṣul by the
late Mr. George Smith in 1875. The text, eighty lines
in length, is inscribed in archaic Assyrian characters
upon both sides of a limestone slab, and was engraved
to commemorate the restoration of a portion of the
temple of the god Ashur in the city of Ashur. The
introductory phrases with which the inscription opens
are the most important part of the text, for they give
the names of the peoples conquered by Adad-nirari
himself, and by his father Pudi-ilu, and by his grandfather Bêl-nirari, and by his great-grandfather Ashur-
uballiṭ. From the information thus furnished it was
found possible to trace in outline the gradual extension
of the Assyrian Empire during a great part of the
fourteenth century B.C.[2]

In the present volume is published for the first time

---

[1] *Cf.* Budge and King, *Annals of the Kings of Assyria*, Vol. I, pp. 1 ff.,
and Introduction, pp. xi ff.

[2] For the text and translation of the memorial slab of Adad-nirari I, see
Annals of the Kings of Assyria, pp. 4 ff. ; photographs of the obverse,
reverse, and edges of the slab are given on pp. xxv, xxix, and xxxiii of that
work.

an inscribed memorial slab of Tukulti-Ninib I, king of Assyria about 1275 B.C., which is very similar to that of his grandfather Adad-nirari I. Like the earlier document, Tukulti-Ninib's slab was engraved to commemorate certain building operations, but instead of merely recording the restoration of a portion of a single temple,[1] it commemorates the founding of a new city, the erection therein of temples to eight deities, the cutting of a canal for the supply of water to the city, the building of a royal palace, and the erection of a wall round the city with the object of rendering it secure against the attacks of enemies. It was on the occasion of the completion of the city wall that the tablet was inscribed. [2]

Another point of resemblance between the memorial slabs of Adad-nirari I and Tukulti-Ninib I may be seen in the fact that the most interesting events recorded by them are not those which they were primarily intended to commemorate; the most important facts are to be found in the introductory portions of the text. We have already noted that Adad-nirari prefixed to the record of his building operations a long genealogy, with lists of the peoples conquered by himself and his forefathers; in like manner Tukulti-

---

[1] Adad-nirari's slab records the rebuilding of a portion of the temple buildings called the *şirlala*; the exact meaning of the word is uncertain. See *Annals of the Kings of Assyria*, p. 7 f., Obv., l. 35—Rev., l. 8.

[2] See below, p. 15.

Ninib, before recounting the founding of his city of Kar-Tukulti-Ninib, supplies valuable information concerning his own military expeditions.

But here the resemblance between the two documents ceases, for whereas the historical information supplied by Adad-nirari is obtained from incidental references in his genealogy,[1] that given by Tukulti-Ninib takes the form of detailed annals, recording the campaigns which he conducted during the course of his reign.[2] In his annals we read, in phrases which remind us of the great cylinder-inscription of Tiglath-pileser I, an account of the gradual conquest of the peoples to the north and east of Assyria, and the record ends with a description of the capture of Babylon and the complete subjugation of Sumer and Akkad.

We already know from a tablet of the "Babylonian Chronicle" that Tukulti-Ninib I conquered Babylonia and ruled the country for seven years until his death, and an inscription of Sennacherib records that this event took place six hundred years before Sennacherib himself captured the city. But Sennacherib does not mention the Babylonian king whom Tukulti-Ninib conquered, and the name of this king has not hitherto been read upon the tablet of the "Babylonian Chronicle" to

---

[1] In Obv., ll. 1–34; cf. *Annals of the Kings of Assyria*, p. 4 ff.

[2] Tukulti-Ninib's titles and genealogy occupy the first eight lines of his inscription; then follow the annals of his campaigns, from Obv., l. 9, to Rev., l. 1.

The Annals of Tukulti-Ninib I, Obverse, ll. 1-14.

which reference has been made.[1] It has been suggested that Bibe,[2] or Bibeiashu, a king of the Third
Dynasty, was the opponent of Tukulti-Ninib I, and
the annals of Tukulti-Ninib I prove that this was so.
They record that Bibeashu, king of Babylon, was
defeated and deported by Tukulti-Ninib I, and they
thus supply another synchronism in Assyrian and
Babylonian history, which is of great value for settling
more definitely the dates of the Babylonian kings of
the Third Dynasty.

Until recently it was believed that Bibe, or Bibeiashu,
lived some sixty or seventy years after Tukulti-Ninib I.
Prof. Hommel in his history placed Tukulti-Ninib I at
about 1300 B.C., and assigned to Bibe's reign the date
1233–1225 B.C.[3] Prof. Delitzsch and Herr Mürdter
assigned the date 1302 (or 1289) B.C. to Tukulti-

---

[1] As a matter of fact this tablet of the " Babylonian Chronicle " (82–7–4,
38) does record the name of Bibeashu as that of the king defeated by
Tukulti-Ninib I. But Mr. Pinches, who first published a translation of the
tablet, and Dr. Winckler, who has edited the text, have both misread the
passage. As my copy and translation of the text differs in several other
points from theirs, I have included in the present work a copy and translation of those lines of the Chronicle which refer to the reign of Tukulti-
Ninib I (see below, Supplementary Texts).

[2] The name is written Bibeashu (*m Bi-be-a-šu*) in the Annals of Tukulti-
Ninib I, and Bibeiashu (*Bi-be-ia-šu*) upon some votive objects found at
Nippur ; the name is abbreviated to Bibe (*m ilu Bi-be*) in the Babylonian
List of Kings.

[3] Hommel, *Geschichte Babyloniens und Assyriens* (in Oncken's
Allgemeine Geschichte), pp. 442, 508.

Ninib I and 1228–1219 B.C. to Bibe,[1] while Prof. Tiele
did not attempt to construct an exact chronology for
the period.[2] During the American diggings at Nippur
three votive objects[3] were found, dedicated to the gods
Bêl and Nusku by a king of the Third, or Kassite,
Dynasty, whose name was Bibeiashu. Dr. Hilprecht
pointed out that the name Bibe, which occurs in the
Babylonian List of Kings, is an abbreviated form of
the name Bibeiashu, and that the two kings were to
be identified with one another, and with a Kassite
king the end of whose name, [ ]*ashu*, is preserved
on a tablet of the " Synchronous History."[4] Assuming
the second identification to be correct, it followed,
from the position of this broken passage in the
" Synchronous History," that a battle between
Bibeiashu and an Assyrian king took place some
time after the agreement made by Adad-nirari I and
Nazi-marattash concerning the boundary between

---

[1] Delitzsch and Mürdter, *Geschichte Babyloniens und Assyriens*,
pp. 93, 265 (Übersicht).

[2] Tiele, *Babylonisch-Assyrische Geschichte*, pp. 138 ff., 147.

[3] They are numbered C.B.M. 8680, 8682, and 8729, and were
published by Hilprecht in *Old Babylonian Inscriptions chiefly from
Nippur* (*Trans. Am. Phil. Soc.*, N.S., xviii, 1), pl. 26, Nos. 70–72.

[4] See Hilprecht, *Old Bab. Inscr.*, p. 11. The tablet of the "Synchronous History" is numbered S. 2106, and a copy of the obverse of the
tablet, on which the passage occurs, is published below, Suppl. Txts. It
will be observed from this copy that not only the end of the name,
𒀸𒋗, has been preserved, but also the beginning 𒁹 𒁉 *i.e.*, Bi[ ],
the first syllable of the name, preceded by the determinative 𒁹.

Assyria and Babylonia. Now the Chronicle 82–7–4, 38 records the conquest of Babylonia by Tukulti-Ninib I, and as he was the grandson of Adad-nirari I, it has been suggested that the opponent of Tukulti-Ninib I was Bibeiashu.[1] The annals of Tukulti-Ninib I, and the new reading of Bibeiashu's name on the Babylonian Chronicle, both confirm this suggestion, and they thus furnish another certain point of contact between Assyrian and Babylonian chronology.

After a short description and analysis of Tukulti-Ninib's text, and a comparison of the class of foundation memorials to which it belongs with the foundation deposits of ancient Egypt, a sketch will be given of the information it supplies on the early history of Assyria.

The tablet upon which the Annals of Tukulti-Ninib I are inscribed is of limestone, and measures $15\frac{7}{8}$ in. in height, $11\frac{1}{4}$ in. to $11\frac{5}{8}$ in. in breadth, and $1\frac{3}{8}$ in. to $1\frac{1}{2}$ in. in thickness. The text is written upon both sides of the tablet, and many of the lines, especially those upon the obverse, run over on to the right hand edge. The lines of the text are separated from each other by lines cut upon the stone by the engraver,[2] and on the reverse similar lines enclose the

---

[1] See Winckler, *Altorientalische Forschungen*, I, pp. 123 ff., and Rogers, *History of Babylonia and Assyria*, I, p. 422.

[2] The spaces left between the lines so cut upon the stone are very regular and only vary between $\frac{3}{8}$ in. and $\frac{1}{2}$ in. ; the majority of the lines are $\frac{3}{8}$ in. in height.

inscription on each side. On the obverse the enclosing
line is omitted from the right side. The obverse
contains thirty-seven lines of the text, and the reverse
thirty lines, and at the end of the reverse a space of
about four lines has been left blank. The text is cut
in bold and clearly formed Assyrian characters. In
the main, the engraver has done his work well and
carefully, but in one or two places he has made
mistakes. It may be noted that in nine passages he
has been obliged to make erasures and has written
the correct characters over the signs he has rubbed
down;[1] and in two passages he has left out a sign
and has not detected the omission.[2] Many of the
characters are archaic, and the forms of some of them
are of great interest.[3] The text is of considerable
value for the study of Assyrian epigraphy, inasmuch

---

[1] See Obv., ll. 7, 18, 29, 35, 36, 37 and Rev., ll. 3, 17, 19; in l. 2 of the
obverse the engraver has omitted the determinative before *Karduniash*,
and has afterwards written it in without making an erasure.

[2] In l. 22 of the obverse the engraver has omitted the sign *ni* from the
verb *u-šik[-ni]-iš*, and in l. 17 of the reverse the sign *bi* from the subs.
taḫ-lu[-bi]-šu.

[3] See especially the forms of KA (Obv., ll. 2, 18, 35, 36), LI (Obv.,
ll. 3, 20, 22, 25, 30, 32, 37, etc.), SAR (Obv., ll. 10, 19), ḲI (Obv., l. 19,
Rev., l. 20), AS (Obv., ll. 23, 31, Rev., l. 24), MUḪ (Obv., l. 27),
GIM (Obv., l. 37), BAD (Rev., ll. 15, 22), LIP (Rev., l. 20), IN (Rev.,
l. 29), 𒀭𒈹 (the ideogram for *Ištar*) in Obv., l. 29, Rev., l. 7, and
SA (the ideogram for *Nabû*) in Rev., l. 12. It will also be seen that two
forms of the sign DU are employed (cp. Obv., l. 6, with Obv., l. 20 and
Rev., l. 18), and also two forms of the sign TA (cp. Obv., ll. 24, 26, and
Rev., l. 4, with Obv., ll. 17 and 22).

The Annals of Tukulti-Ninib I, Obverse, ll. 14–26.

as it exhibits the style of Assyrian characters employed in monumental inscriptions in the early part of the thirteenth century B.C.

The text inscribed upon the tablet falls into four main divisions, which may be enumerated as follows :— I. The introduction, giving the king's titles and genealogy ; II. The record of the king's military expeditions; III. The account of the building of the city of Kar-Tukulti-Ninib ; and IV. The conclusion, containing a blessing and curses intended to protect the city wall and the king's memorial tablet. The following is a more detailed analysis of the inscription arranged under the above four headings :—

I. INTRODUCTION.

Obv., ll.   1–7 :   The king's name and titles.
   „   l.   8 :   His genealogy.

II. THE MILITARY EXPEDITIONS.

Obv., ll. 9–13 :   His first campaign against the Kutî and the inhabitants of four other districts.
   „   ll. 14–18 :   His conquest of Shubarî and ten other districts.
   „   ll. 19–27 :   His subjugation of forty kings of the lands of Na'iri.
   „   l. 28–Rev., l. 1 :   His defeat of Bibeashu, and his conquest of Sumer and Akkad.

II. The building of Kar-Tukulti-Ninib.

Rev., ll. 2–5 : The occasion of the founding of the city by the king.

„ ll. 6–8 : His building of temples to the gods therein.

„ ll. 8–11 : His cutting of a canal thereto, and the appointment of offerings for the gods.

„ ll. 11–14 : His building of a mound within the city, and the erection of a palace thereon.

„ ll. 15–17 : His building of a wall round the city, and the setting in place of his memorial tablet.

IV. Conclusion.

Rev., ll. 18–21 : Appeal to future rulers to keep the city wall in repair and his tablet in its place, and a blessing on those that do so.

„ ll. 22–30 : Curses on anyone who shall destroy the city wall, or shall remove his memorial tablet, or shall deface his name, or shall neglect or destroy the city.

The occasion on which the memorial tablet was inscribed was the completion of the wall round the city of Kar-Tukulti-Ninib. This is clear from the opening lines of the concluding section of the text, which read : " In the days that are to come, when this " wall shall have grown old and shall have fallen into " ruins, may a future prince repair the damaged parts " thereof, and may he anoint my memorial tablet, and " may he offer sacrifices and restore it unto its place, " and then Ashur will hearken unto his prayers." [1] In the lines which precede this passage the building of the city wall had been recorded, and we may therefore conclude that the memorial tablet was buried in a small recess or cavity within the wall, or possibly embedded in its foundations. The king's object was to make certain that his fame as the founder of the city and the builder of its fortifications should not be forgotten.

The custom of building up inscribed memorial tablets, cones, and cylinders within the walls and in the foundations of palaces and temples was practised by both Babylonian and Assyrian kings, and to it we owe much of our knowledge of the history of the two countries. The Babylonian and Assyrian employed two words for their building inscriptions. The word used for the inscribed cylinders of clay which were buried in the walls near entrances, and perhaps in the foundations

---

[1] Rev., ll. 18-21.

of a palace or temple, is always *temennu*. The second word is *narû*, and this is always used of inscriptions upon stone. It could be applied to rock inscriptions, such as those near Bavian and Behistun, or to inscribed monoliths, which were set up in conspicuous positions, or to smaller inscribed stones of irregular shape. But the most numerous class of inscriptions, which were termed *narê*, are stone tablets, such as that of Tukulti-Ninib I, which are comparatively small in size, and are inscribed on both sides. It is clear that these were not fixed in any way to the face of a wall, for they bear no trace of fastenings, and, had they been intended for this purpose, they would not have been inscribed upon the back. Those that record the erection of a building, such as a temple or a palace, may possibly have been deposited in a sanctuary or in an archive chamber; but where the record concerns the building of a city wall no such chamber would be available.

It therefore seems to me more probable that in all cases the tablet was not left lying in a room, where it might easily be damaged or carried off, but was built up in the wall or in the foundations of the building, probably in a box of clay or stone, or within a small recess or hollow lined with burnt brick. Such a plan would ensure the presence in the building of a permanent memorial to its founder; and it was probably in consequence of their having been preserved beneath or within the actual framework of the building that

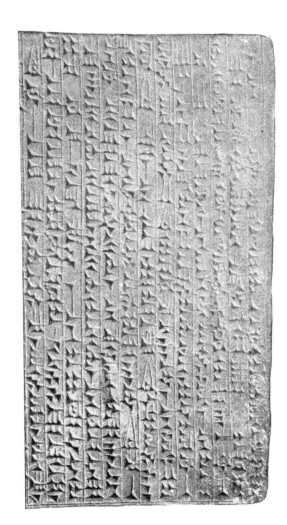

The Annals of Tukulti-Ninib I, Obverse, ll. 25–37.

later kings, when clearing the site of a ruined temple, sometimes recovered the *narê*, or memorial tablets, of their predecessors who had founded or restored the building. In the event of the building falling into ruins, the recess in which the tablet had been laid at its foundation would be " its place," to which the king in his inscription on the *narû* always prays his successors to restore it. This the later king is implored to do, after he has anointed the stone with oil, and has offered the duly appointed sacrifices to appease the gods and to obtain their protection. The anointing with oil no doubt possessed a ceremonial signification, and also tended to preserve the surface of the stone.

The custom of burying memorial tablets may, perhaps, be said to find its equivalent in Egypt in the groups of foundation deposits which have been found in recent years among the remains of ancient cities. The most complete Egyptian foundation deposits that have yet been recovered belong to the Ptolemaic and Saite periods, and these were the first deposits that were discovered ; but since then they have been found in Egyptian buildings of all periods, extending back to the Fifth Dynasty. Unlike the Babylonian and Assyrian clay cylinders and foundation memorials, the Egyptian foundation deposits consist of a number of different kinds of objects which may be classified under the following headings : (1) pottery, consisting of libation vases and cups for offerings, and often models of the

same ; under this heading may also be set the models of
corn-grinders and mortars which are often found ;
(2) models of tools used in building operations, generally
made of bronze, but sometimes having wooden handles ;
(3) specimens of building materials, including models of
mud bricks, specimens of mortar, pieces of gold, silver,[1]
lead, copper, iron and precious stones, cut into the form
of small plaques, and often engraved with the name of
the king who erected the building ; and (4) small objects
of glazed faïence, generally consisting of models of
animal offerings ; this last class of deposit is generally
found in temples of the Middle and Late Empires, and
rarely in Ptolemaic buildings.

As a good specimen of a single foundation deposit we
give in the note below a list of the contents of a deposit
from those found in the great temenos at Naucratis.[2]

---

[1] Sometimes in the Ptolemaic period actual pieces of gold and silver
were not used, but imitations were put in their place. For instance, at
Koptos, in foundation deposits of the Ptolemaic period, gold is represented
by gilt blocks of sandstone, and silver by a piece of wood thinly plated ;
see Petrie, *Koptos*, p. 19.

[2] A deposit from those found at Naukratis consists of models of two
libation vases and four cups for offerings, all made of glazed ware, models
of a pair of corn-grinders of sandstone, and of a limestone mortar, and
models of a bronze knife and long-handled axe ; all these objects probably
had a ceremonial significance. The models of tools consisted of an iron
hoe and mortar rake with wooden handle, and a bronze adze, chisel,
mortar trowel, and hatchet, and four alabaster pegs (possibly models of
pegs used in marking out a site). The building materials consisted of a
model of a mud brick, a plaque of green glazed ware, and plaques of gold,

We may also cite the sets of foundation deposits from Gemayemi,[1] and those of Psammetichus I from Tell Dafna,[2] of Amasis II from Tell Nebesha,[3] of Thothmes III and Usertesen I from Abydos,[4] and of

silver, lead, copper, iron, turquoise, jasper, pale lapis-lazuli and agate, and chips of more valuable stones, comprising the richest blue lapis, red jasper, green turquoise, and translucent obsidian. Finally the deposit included a cartouche-plaque of lapis-lazuli engraved on both sides with the name of Ptolemy Philadelphus (see Petrie, *Naukratis*, I p. 29 f.). Fine deposits of the Ptolemaic period have also been found in the temenos built by Philip Arrhidaeus at Tûkh el Ḳaramûṣ (see *Tell el-Yahûdîyeh*, p. 55).

[1] In the Third Egyptian Room, Case K, No. 150. They are of the Ptolemaic or perhaps the Saite period, and were found in the north-west corner of the great building at Tell Gemayemi.

[2] Foundation deposits of Psammetichus I (about B.C. 650) were found in the corners of the fort at Tell Dafna. They consist of plaques, most of them inscribed with the king's name, made of gold, silver, lead, copper, carnelian, green felspar, lapis-lazuli, jasper, and green glazed faïence ; mud bricks, lead and copper ore, a model of a libation cup, and a full sized corn-grinder of limestone. Specimens of the deposit are exhibited in the Third Egyptian Room in the British Museum, Table-case K, No. 149.

[3] The foundation deposit exhibited in the Third Egyptian Room, Table-case K, No. 151, is from the south-west corner of the smaller temple at Tell Nebesha, and consists of plaques of precious metals and stones inscribed with the titles of Amasis II (about B.C. 550). In addition to the plaques, models of metal, stone, and pottery vessels were found in the deposits from this temple.

[4] Those of Thothmes III (about B.C. 1530) consist of bronze models of tools found in the temple of Osiris at Abydos (British Museum, No. 37324). Of the tools two chisels and an axe-head are inscribed with the king's name. Still more important are the plaques from foundation deposits of Usertesen I (about B.C. 2430), which were also found at Abydos (British Museum, Nos. 38076-8). The plaques are of bronze, marble, and faïence, and are inscribed with the king's name ; what is unique about them is that they are embedded in the centre of mud bricks, possibly with a view to their preservation.

Queen Hâtshepset from Dêr el-Baharî,[1] which are preserved in the British Museum.

While the Babylonian and Assyrian foundation memorials were chiefly intended to preserve the name of the king and the record of his building operations, the object of the Egyptian foundation deposits seems to have been of a purely magical nature. It will have been seen that many of the objects found in the deposits represent the materials and implements employed in the actual work of the building: such are the models of tools and bricks and the specimens of building materials; the gold and precious stones representing the materials employed in mosaic work and in the decorations of the shrine. The remaining objects found in the deposits may for the most part be connected with a ceremonial or sacrificial object, e.g., the pottery, the models of libation cups, the mortars and corn-grinders, and some of the bronze models of knives and axes.[2] We may therefore conclude that the Egyptian deposits were closely connected with a religious ceremony and sacrifice carried out at the laying of the temple's foundations.

---

[1] Of the set of foundation deposits of Queen Hâtshepset from Dêr el-Baharî, and exhibited in the Third Egyptian Room, No. 280 (wall-case), the model of the wooden clamp used to fasten limestone blocks together, and what is probably the model of a sledge for transporting stone, are of great interest.

[2] The little brick of myrrh, from a foundation deposit of uncertain date at El-Kâb (see Quibell, *El Kab*, p. 16), is probably of a ceremonial character.

The Annals of Tukulti-Ninib I, Reverse, ll. 1–14.

This conclusion is supported by the fact that skulls of oxen have been found in deposits possibly dating from the Fifth Dynasty at Abydos, and in the deposits of Usertesen I at the same site were the bones and heads of oxen ;[1] also in the south-east corner of the fort at Dafna were some teeth and bones of an ox with a foundation deposit of Psammetichus I.[2] Similarly in a deposit in the Ramesseum a bone from a calf's foot was found,[3] and the bones of a calf were also discovered in the south-east deposit in the Ptolemaic temenos at Tûkh el-Karamûs.[4] We may also note that in the south-west corner of the building of the fort at Dafna, in a small cylindrical hole below the base of the brickwork, were found charcoal and the burnt bones of a small bird (probably a pigeon), which were evidently the remains of a foundation sacrifice.

In connection with these actual remains of animals and birds, may be mentioned the models of animal offerings made of glazed faïence and found among the smaller objects in foundation deposits of the Middle Empire.   Thus in the temples of Ta-usert and of Sa-Ptaḥ, at Thebes, were found representations of the heads and haunches of bulls, oxen beheaded and with their legs tied together ready for sacrifice, a calf's head,

[1] See *Abydos*, II, p. 20.
[2] See *Tanis*, II (*Tell Defenneh*), p. 55.
[3] See Quibell, *Ramesseum*, p. 6.
[4] See *Tell el-Yahûdîyeh*, p. 55.

and figures of fish, ducks, and a pigeon.[1] Similar
models of the heads of bulls and calves, and of the
haunches and bodies of bulls, have been found in
deposits of Rameses III and of Apries, at Abydos,[2] and
others in the Ramesseum and at El-Kâb.[3] It may be
concluded that these models of animal offerings are
to be connected with the foundation sacrifice, and an
explanation of them is attempted below.

Professor Petrie suggested that the models of stone
and metal libation vessels and pottery found in the
foundation deposits were cheap substitutes for more
valuable vessels, which were deposited in earlier times
under temples after they had been used in the foundation
ceremony, in order to prevent their being used again.
Similarly the models of tools have been explained as
representing the actual tools which had already been
used in the foundation ceremony and would otherwise
have been forfeit to the gods.[4] But this suggestion
leaves unexplained the specimens of building materials
and the plaques of precious stones and metals, for these
represent materials employed and placed permanently
in the structure of the temple, and they cannot in any
sense be declared forfeit to the gods, to whose service
they were already dedicated.

---

[1] See Petrie, *Six Temples at Thebes*, p. 14 f. and pl. XVI.
[2] See *Abydos*, II, p. 19 and I, p. 32.
[3] See Quibell, *Ramesseum*, p. 6, and *El Kab*, p. 16.
[4] See *Tanis*, II (*Tell Nebesheh*), p. 15.

No satisfactory explanation has yet been offered of the meaning and object of the Egyptian foundation deposits, but the inquiry may perhaps be forwarded by considering the origin of the buildings under the walls of which they are generally found. The Egyptian temple in one of its primitive forms was merely a mortuary chapel attached to the tomb of the deceased, and it is possible that in their primitive state the foundation deposits were placed under its walls in much the same way that *ushabti* figures were placed in the tomb itself near the body of the dead man. As it was believed that the latter would do the work of the deceased and serve him in the future life, so it is conceivable that the foundation deposits were buried in order to furnish him with materials and implements for any building operations he might desire to carry out.[1] The models of animal offerings would supply him with animals for the foundation sacrifice, whose bones he would bury, as we find the actual skulls and bones of bulls and calves buried under the foundations of buildings during later periods. Similarly the models of libation vases and sacrificial knives, and the mortars and corn-grinders

---

[1] In support of this theory it may be noted that a deposit found at El-Kâb included a green glazed figure like a *ushabti* (see Quibell, *El Kab*, p. 16). The amulets, in the form of wooden models of girdle-ties, found at El-Kâb (*op. cit.*, pl. XXI, No. 10), and in a scattered deposit of Thothmes III at Nubt (see Petrie and Quibell, *Naqada and Ballas*, p. 68), would also seem to have a personal significance.

would furnish him with other necessary adjuncts to the
ceremony. In course of time the original significance
of the deposits may have been forgotten, although the
custom of burying them was still continued. In the
Ptolemaic period the burying of models of animal
offerings seems to have been discontinued, and the
other deposits were placed not only under the walls of
temples, but also under those of secular buildings, such
as the fort at Dafna.

Whatever their origin, it will be seen that the
Egyptian foundation deposits in many respects present
a contrast to the foundation cylinders and memorial
tablets of the Babylonians and Assyrians. It is true
that the inscribed plaques preserve the name of the
founder of the building under which they are ⋅buried,
but as a whole the Egyptian deposits seem to be of a
purely magical nature. A closer Babylonian parallel
may perhaps be seen in the small clay figures of demi-
gods or good spirits in human form, and the clay models
of birds, which are buried in clay boxes near entrances
in Babylonian temples, a foot or two below the surface
of the pavement. Sometimes bones are found lying in
the bottom of the boxes in which the models of the
birds are buried. The burial of these little models may
have had some connection with the religious ceremony
at the foundation of the temple, and it is probable that
the little human figures at any rate were believed to be
potent for guarding the entrance from the approach

The Annals of Tukulti-Ninib I, Reverse, ll. 14–26,

of devils.[1] If this were so, their origin and object would differ from those suggested above for the Egyptian foundation deposits.

Of the Babylonian and Assyrian foundation memorials we know that the *temennê*, or inscribed clay cylinders, were often, if not always, built into the unburnt brick in the interior of the walls on either side of entrances, but the place, and, to some extent, the manner in which the *narê*, or stone memorial tablets, were buried is still to a great extent a matter for conjecture. That at least in some instances the tablets were enclosed in coffers of stone or clay is proved by two memorial tablets of Ashur-nasir-pal (B.C. 885—B.C. 860) and the so-called "Sun-god Tablet" of Nabû-pal-iddina (about B.C. 870), which were found in the coffers in which they were originally buried. The two tablets of Ashur-nasir-pal, British Museum, Nos. 90,980 and 90,981, which record

---

[1] That the little clay figures, though in human shape, are the figures of divine beings, is proved by an inscription upon the back of one of them, which was found by Drs. Koldewey and Andrae buried in a clay box below the threshold of the temple of Ninib at Babylon. The little figure is that of a bearded man, who wore a copper girdle and carried a gold staff about three inches long in his hand. I found time last Christmas (1903) to ride down to Ḳal'a Sherḳât for a couple of nights and pay a visit to Dr. Andrae, and while I was there he showed me a careful drawing he had made of the signs inscribed upon the figure. The inscription reads: *sukkal* (𒀭𒇽𒇽) *ili-ia mu-'i-ir-ru ḫa-mi-[iṭ?] zêr šadêᵖˡ(e)*, "Minister of my god, the Director, the swift one (?), the seed of the mountains." The lines evidently contain a description of the little figure, and show that he was regarded as a servant of the god Ninib, in whose temple he was buried.

the founding of the temple of Makhir, in the city of Imgur-Bêl, were found in the limestone coffer in which they were originially buried, British Museum, No. 73. The same inscription, recording the building of the temple, is engraved on each of the tablets, and in a shorter form upon the coffer.[1] The "Sun-god Tablet"[2] was made by Nabû-pal-iddina to record his restoration of E-babbara, the temple of the Sun-god at Sippar. It was found in a clay box or coffer, buried about three feet below the asphalt pavement of a chamber in the temple at Abû-Habba. It is probable that the chamber had been originally paved with burnt bricks, which had been removed, leaving only the asphalt in which they had originally been bedded. The tablet had not lain undisturbed since the time of Nabû-pal-iddina, for in the box with it were found clay impressions of the scene sculptured upon the tablet, one of which bears an inscription of Nabopolassar (B.C. 625–604);[3] also two baked clay cylinders of Nabonidus (B.C. 555–538) were found in the box with it. It is clear therefore that both Nabopolassar and Nabonidus each in turn came across Nabû-pal-iddina's tablet in the course of rebuilding

---

[1] For a translation of the inscription, see Budge and King, *Annals of the Kings of Assyria*, Vol. I, pp. 167 ff.

[2] British Museum, No. 91,000. The text of the tablet is published in *Cun. Inscr. West. Asia*, Vol. V, pl. 60 f.

[3] The inscription on the clay impression has been published by Jastrow, *American Journal of Semitic Languages and Literatures*, Vol. XV (1899), pp. 65 ff.

the temple of the Sun-god, and each in turn restored it " unto its place," burying it again with due honour. It is probable that the clay box it which it was found was not made by Nabû-pal-iddina, but dates from Nabopolassar's reign.[1] The above two examples show that at any rate in some cases the *narû* was protected by a stone coffer or clay box before it was built up in the structure of the wall or buried under the pavement of a chamber. No statistics are yet available for determining in what part of the Babylonian or Assyrian building the *narê* were placed, but a good deal has been noted and published with regard to the position and manner of burial of foundation deposits in Egyptian buildings. A sketch of the character of these deposits has already been given, and their object has been discussed and compared with that of their Babylonian and Assyrian equivalents. The description of them may here be supplemented by giving a short summary of what is known with regard to the positions in which they have been found and the manner in which they are buried.

---

[1] In this connection it may be noted that the three bronze statues of Gudea grasping inscribed bronze cones (British Museum, Nos. 91,056–91,058), which were presented to the British Museum by Mr. J. F. Streatfeild, were purchased by him from a native, who told him they were found with some clay cones bricked up in a niche in a wall of a chamber at Tell Loh. The cones were inserted into the walls of the niche with their heads protruding. It is unfortunate that more exact details as to the find have not been preserved.

d

The Egyptian foundation deposits are generally found in the corners of a building and under the actual wall. Thus at Naukratis four foundation deposits, all alike, were found under each corner of the great temenos, and smaller deposits were found under two of the corners of the central hall.[1] Two instances are known of buildings in which deposits were placed under only three of the corners. Thus in the smaller temple at Nebesha, built by Amasis II, B.C. 572, deposits were found in the brick-containing wall of the foundation under all the corners except the north-east one. As a double set of foundation plaques was found in the deposit in the south-west corner, it was suggested by Prof. Petrie that through accident the north-east corner might not have been prepared properly, and the surplus deposits put in the south-west corner.[2] But we meet with the same arrangement in the principal building at Gemayemi (of the Ptolemaic or perhaps the Saite period),[3] so that the suggestion that the arrangement was due to accident is scarcely probable. Generally the deposits are buried under the actual wall, but in some instances they are found within the walls in the corners under the pavement.[4] In addition to their usual places

---

[1] See *Naukratis*, I, pp. 28, 32.

[2] See *Tanis*, II (*Tell Nebesheh*), p. 14.

[3] See *Tanis*, II (*Gemaiyemi*), p. 39 f.

[4] Thus at Gemayemi the centre of each deposit was about 30 inches from each wall, and 18 inches deep, *i.e.*, at a level of four or five feet above the base of the wall.

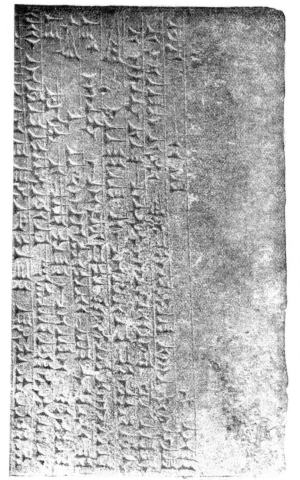

The Annals of Tukulti-Ninib I, Reverse, ll. 23-30.

in the corners, deposits were also found both at Nebesha
and Gemayemi under the centre of the building, and in
the temples built at Thebes by Ta-usert and her husband
Sa-Ptah, a king of the Nineteenth Dynasty, they occur
not only in the corners but also along the walls of
chambers and under doorways.[1]

The deposits are usually found in small rectangular
or circular pits which were cut in the ground before the
wall was built. At Naukratis rectangular pits were cut
in the ground beneath the stones which lined the wall
on the inside of the building, and after the deposits
were placed in them the holes were filled up with yellow
sand, which was also spread in a layer a few inches
deep under the foundations of the walls. At Koptos
circular pits were cut in the clay on which the building
stood, and in the temple of Amen-hetep II at Thebes
the pits are cut out of the rock. Sometimes two
foundation pits are found in each corner of a building,
as in the small temple of Thothmes III at El-Kâb.
Here one pit is set exactly in the corner, and the
second one is a metre's distance from it along the side
wall.[2]

The filling of the pits with sand after the foundation
deposits had been placed in them was practised not
only in Ptolemaic times but also under the Middle and

---

[1] See Petrie, *Six Temples at Thebes*, p. 14.
[2] See Quibell, *El-Kab*, p. 25, and pl. XXVI.

Early Empires. We can trace the practice back to the Fifth Dynasty, for in some pits at Abydos, probably dating from this period, sand is found, while others had been filled in with the brown muddy earth which had been dug out of the holes.[1] Usually the deposits were only protected by the sand or earth with which the pits were filled, but some foundation-pits in the Ramesseum were covered with great sandstone blocks cut and painted with cartouches of Rameses II.[2] Pits were not always used for the foundation deposits, as in a building of Rameses III at Abydos, where they were placed in a deep bed of sand spread above earlier remains on which the building was constructed.[3] And it has been suggested that foundation deposits may sometimes have been buried, not in pits, but in stone boxes sunk into the ground, but there is little evidence to prove that this was so.[4]

Generally the pits are not lined or floored in any way, but in some foundation pits in the Ramesseum floors of mud bricks were found, not at the bottom, but half way down the pit. The bulk of the deposit was found below

---

[1] See *Abydos*, II, p. 20.

[2] See Quibell, *Ramesseum*, p. 6.

[3] See *Abydos*, II, p. 19.

[4] Near the door at the east end of a temple of the Middle Kingdom at Koptos was found a sandstone box, which, as it bore chisel marks both inside and out, was probably not intended to be seen, but may have been originally buried, and it is possible that it once contained foundation deposits; see Petrie, *Koptos*, p. 11.

these floors, which thus acted as a protection, and in all cases the rest of the pit was filled up with clean sand.[1] It is hard to trace any system or order in the arrangement in the pit of the objects forming the foundation deposits. In Ptolemaic times at any rate it is probable that the chips of precious stones and fragments of building materials were placed in glazed cups to keep them together and arranged in order in the pit. In the Middle Empire the models of tools are sometimes found under a reed mat, on which rests a block of limestone engraved with cartouches of the builder, and above the limestone block are found numbers of small objects of glazed faïence. But no order or system seems to have been followed in their arrangement. They have the appearance of having been poured into the pit without regard to their relative positions.

From the preceding paragraphs it will be clear that a good deal of information has already been accumulated with regard to the manner in which the Egyptian foundation deposits were buried, and it is to be hoped that it will not be long before similar information is obtained concerning the burial of Babylonian and Assyrian foundation memorials. In Tukulti-Ninib's memorial tablet it may be noted that in ll. 17, 20 and 22 of the reverse he speaks of only one *narû*, not of *narê* in the plural, but it does not follow from this that

---

[1] See Quibell, *Ramesseum*, p. 6.

only one tablet was inscribed and placed in or under the wall, the building of which the inscription records. It is clear that the city of Kar-Tukulti-Ninib was of considerable size, and it is probable that tablets similar to the one that has been recovered were bricked in or buried at several points in the wall around the city.[1]

The existence of the city of Kar-Tukulti-Ninib was already known from the tablet of the "Babylonian Chronicle," which gives an account of his reign ; for it is there recorded that it was in this city the king met his death. The Chronicle recounts how his son Ashur-nasir-pal headed a revolt of the nobles of Assyria against his father. Tukulti-Ninib took refuge in the city of Kar-Tukulti-Ninib, but they surrounded him in a house within the city, and on capturing him put him to death. The memorial tablet does not tell us at what period of his reign the king founded the city, but from the extensive building operations he carried out there, it is clear that the building of the city must have extended over several years of his reign. This may be concluded from the fact that he erected temples in the city dedicated to the gods Ashur, and Adad, and Shamash, and Ninib, and Nusku, and Nergal, and Imina-bi, and to the goddess Ishtar. He

---

[1] Each tablet, on this supposition, would have borne the same inscription, the singular *narû* in each case referring to the tablet on which it is inscribed.

Upper half.   *Lower half.*

The Annals of Tukulti-Ninib I, Right side.

also cut a canal for the supply of water from the Tigris to the interior of the city, and he constructed a high mound upon which be built his palace. And finally he fortified the city by building a high wall round it. It is not improbable that he founded the city in the early years of his reign, and that he continued to enrich and strengthen it when he returned to Assyria in the intervals between his various campaigns.

In his annals Tukulti-Ninib does not number his campaigns, nor, with the exception of the first, does he state in which year of his reign they took place. He describes his expeditions in four successive paragraphs of his inscription, and it is probable that to a great extent his conquests are enumerated on a geographical basis, and not necessarily in the order in which they were made. His first campaign is recorded in ll. 9–13 of the obverse of the memorial tablet, and in the opening words of the paragraph it is described as having taken place "in the beginning of my sovereignty, in the first year of my reign." It was directed against the Kutî and the inhabitants of four other districts.

The second paragraph, consisting of ll. 14–18 of the obverse of the tablet, records the conquest of eleven districts, enumerated by name, of which "the broad extent of the land of Shubarî" may probably be regarded as the most important. The paragraph is introduced by the vague phrase *i-na u-mi-šu-ma*, "at that time," which, following as it does the account of his first expedition, may perhaps indicate that the districts were subdued in the earlier rather than in the latter part of his reign. The conquest of "forty kings of the lands of Na'iri" is the subject of the third paragraph (ll. 19–27). This section follows the preceding one without any indication of time, and is introduced only by a reference to the difficult nature of the country traversed. It is possible that the conquest of the forty kings was not achieved in one campaign, but was effected during several expeditions the total results of which are here grouped together.

The fourth paragraph (Obv., l. 28—Rev., l. 1) describes the defeat of Bibeashu, king of Babylon, and the complete subjugation of Sumer and Akkad. From the tablet of the "Babylonian Chronicle," to which reference has already been made,[1] we know that Tukulti-Ninib ruled in Babylonia for seven years, until "the nobles of " Akkad and Karduniash revolted and set Adad-shum-" usur upon his father's throne." What interval there was between this revolt and that of Ashur-nasir-pal, another of Tukulti-Ninib's sons, who succeeded in slaying his father and seating himself on the Assyrian throne, the Chronicle does not say. But it is not unlikely that the troubles in Babylonia and Assyria were contemporaneous, or at any rate that they followed swiftly upon one another. If this were so, the conquest

---

[1] No. 82-7-4, 38 ; see above, pp. 4 and 7.

of Babylonia by Tukulti-Ninib I would fall some eight years before the end of his reign. In any case we may conclude that he did not turn his attention to the subjugation of the Southern Kingdom until he had secured himself against the attacks of other foes.

In addition to the detailed record of his campaigns, the king's principal conquests are commemorated in the royal titles with which the inscription opens. Here the order in which the districts are enumerated is different to that adopted in the four paragraphs which follow. The titles "the king of Karduniash, the king of Sumer and Akkad," naturally head the list of foreign conquests and follow the titles "the king of Assyria, the king of the four quarters (of the world)." In the title "the king of the Shubarî and the Ḳutî," the order of the paragraphs is reversed, possibly because Shubarî was considered the more important of the two regions. "The king of all the lands of Na'iri" occupies the last place in the list of titles, and with reference to the Shubarî and the Ḳutî its position in the list corresponds to that which it occupies in the more detailed account.

Tukulti-Ninib's first campaign was directed against the peoples inhabiting the region to the east of Assyria. The most important district which he conquered on this expedition was that of the Ḳutî, which may with some probability be placed to the east of the Lower Zâb.[1]

---

[1] See Delitzsch, *Paradies*, p. 233 f.

The Ḳutî had already been subdued by Adad-nirari I [1] and Pudi-ilu,[2] Tukulti-Ninib's grandfather and great-grandfather, but it is clear they were a warlike tribe, and on the first opportunity regained their independence. The Uḳumanî and the lands of Elkhunia and Sharnida and Mekhri are described as mountainous, and probably lay in about the same region as the Ḳutî, possibly to the north of the Lower Zâb. Of these districts Mekhri was conquered at a later period by Tiglath-pileser I.[3] and again by Ashur-naṣir-pal II.[4]

The country took its name from the mekhru-tree, probably a pine or fir, which grew there, and it is interesting to note that the name of the country is written at the time of Ashur-naṣir-pal as *mât* ^{isu} *me-iḫ-ri* ^{pl}, "the land of the mekhru-trees." The trees found in the country seem to have been highly prized, for when he conquered the land, Ashur-naṣir-pal brought back beams of mekhru-wood for the temple of Ishtar at Nineveh. In the tablet of Tiglath-pileser I the land of Mekhri is mentioned in connection with the conquest of the land of [Kuma]ni, var. [Ḳuma]nî, a name which is restored from l. 18 of the same tablet, where "twenty thousand

---

[1] See Budge and King, *Annals of the Kings of Assyria*, p. 5.
[2] *Op. cit.*, p. 6.
[3] On one of his tablets Tiglath-pileser I says that he conquered "[the "land of Ḳuma]ni as far as the mountain (or better, land) of Mekhri (var. "Mikhri)"; see Budge and King, *Annals of the Kings of Assyria*, p. 119, l. 13.
[4] See *Annals of the Kings of Assyria*, p. 374, col. III, l. 91 f.

troops of the land of Ḳuma[ni]" are mentioned.[1] From the association of Mekhri with Ḳumanî by Tiglath-pileser I, and of Mekhri with Uḳumanî by Tukulti-Ninib I, it may perhaps be inferred that *Ḳumanî* and *Uḳumanî* are variant names for the same district. In the account of this first campaign it is interesting to note that the conquered peoples are stated to have brought their yearly tribute to the city of Ashur, and not to Calah, which had been built and established as the capital by Shalmaneser I, Tukulti-Ninib's father. It may therefore be inferred that Tukulti-Ninib restored the ancient city of Ashur to her former position as the capital of the kingdom.

Of the eleven conquered districts enumerated in the second paragraph describing the campaigns, it is probable that the land of Shubarî, which occurs last in the list, was regarded as the most important. This may be inferred partly from the reference to its broad extent,[2] but chiefly from the fact that it is singled out for special mention in the list of the king's titles which precedes the account of the campaigns. A proof that the inhabitants of this district, like those of Ḳutî, were a powerful and warlike race may be seen in the necessity

---

[1] See *Annals of the Kings of Assyria*, p. 120. *Cf.* also K. 2807, another tablet of Tiglath-pileser I, where certain cities are mentioned in the land of Ḳu[. . . .], which may probably be restored as Ḳu[manî], see *Annals*, p. 121.

[2] See l. 17 f.

for their reconquest by Tukulti-Ninib I, although his grandfather, Adad-nirari I, had already subdued them.[1]

The ten other conquered districts enumerated in the second paragraph are the lands of Kurṭî, Kummukhi, Pushshe, Mumme, Alzi, Madani, Nikhani, Alaia, Tearzi, and Purukuzzi. The first two districts on the list, the lands of Kurṭî and Kummukhi, are also closely associated by Tiglath-pileser I, who relates that the forces of the Kurṭê came to the rescue of the men of Kummukhi when the latter had been defeated by him.[2] The districts lay to the north-west of Assyria, on the borders of Northern Syria. Pushshe is mentioned on a fragment of an early Assyrian bowl, which may possibly have borne an inscription of Tukulti-Ninib I himself.[3] The lands of Alzi and Purukuzzu are also coupled together by Tiglath-pileser I, who relates that he brought them again into subjection to Assyria after they had been held for fifty years by the land of Mushki (Meshech).[4] He also mentions them in connection with the land of Shubarî. It is probable that all the districts enumerated in the second paragraph lay in the region to the north-west of Assyria.

The third paragraph records in general terms the defeat of " forty kings of the lands of Na'iri." In like

---

[1] See *Annals of the Kings of Assyria*, p. 5.
[2] *Op. cit.*, pp. 40, 51 ff.
[3] No. 56-9-9, 162 ; see Appendix, p. 136 f.
[4] See *Annals of the Kings of Assyria*, pp. 35, 47.

manner Tiglath-pileser I defeated "twenty-three kings of the land of Na'iri," and he gives all the separate districts over which they ruled by name,[1] and a little later on, in the Cylinder Inscription, he records his pursuit of "sixty kings of the lands of Na'iri."[2] The name *Na'iri* was a general term for the mountainous districts to the north of Assyria, extending well to the west of Lake Van, and probably eastwards to the districts bordering on Lake Urmi. It will be seen that the conquests of Tukulti-Ninib enumerated in the first three paragraphs led to the subjugation of the territory to the north, and to the north-west, and to the east of Assyria; and it is probable that the campaigns occupied the earlier years of his reign, and were undertaken with the object of rendering his country secure against attack from these quarters when he concentrated his forces for operations against Babylon.

These operations resulted in the most important conquest of Tukulti-Ninib. They are recorded in the fourth paragraph, which relates how he defeated Bibeashu, the Kassite king of Babylon, and brought the whole of Sumer and Akkad into subjection to the Assyrian crown. Some details concerning this campaign and its results are already known to us from the

---

[1] See *Annals of the Kings of Assyria*, p. 66 f.
[2] *Op. cit.*, p. 68.

Babylonian Chronicle, No. 82–7–4, 38.[1] This document
tells us that after defeating Bibeashu, Tukulti-Ninib
destroyed the city-wall of Babylon and put many of the
inhabitants to the sword. He despoiled Babylon of her
riches, including the treasures of E-sagil, the great
temple of Marduk, and carried away to Assyria the
statue of the god himself. He then proceeded to
appoint his own officers, and established his own system
of administration in the capital. From Tukulti-Ninib's
own annals we further learn that he carried Bibeashu
away to Assyria, and led him a prisoner and in chains
before Ashur, the national god.

The deportation of Bibeashu, the Babylonian king,
was the symbol of the complete subjugation of the
southern kingdom, and this was emphasized by the
removal to Assyria of the great statue of Marduk, the
national god of Babylon. Assyria had for centuries
outgrown her dependence on the Southern Kingdom
and had thrown off the Babylonian yoke, but, so far as
we know, it was not until the reign of Tukulti-Ninib I
that she succeeded in capturing Babylon and in sub-
jugating Sumer and Akkad. Tukulti-Ninib's reign thus
marks an epoch in Assyrian and Babylonian history.

---

[1] The portion of the Chronicle relating to Tukulti-Ninib's conquest and
occupation of Babylon is translated below; see Supplementary Texts,
No. 1. No. 2 of the Supplementary Texts gives the few signs that remain
of the corresponding account in the " Synchronous History," with the
context in which they occur; see above, p. 8.

Portion of a Babylonian Chronicle referring to the reign of Tukulti-Ninib I.

[82–7–4, 38, Col. IV, ll. 1–13.]

In order to illustrate the significance of his conquest, we may here briefly summarize what is at present known of the early struggles of Assyria, which were at first directed to obtain her independence and afterwards to extend her empire on the south. From this summary it will be seen how the conquests of his predecessors paved Tukulti-Ninib's way and made it possible for him to conquer Babylon and govern her for seven years.

Up to the present time not very much information has been obtained with regard to the early history of Assyria, but, so far as our knowledge goes, we see Assyria first as part and parcel of the Babylonian kingdom, and later on governed by viceroys owing allegiance to Babylon, and afterwards ruled by independent kings. In the reign of Gudea, king of Shirpurla, when the Sumerians were still the predominant race in Babylonia, it is probable that the cities which later on formed the nucleus of the Assyrian empire were subject to their southern neighbours, for Gudea records that he rebuilt the temple of the goddess Ninni (Ishtar) in Ninâ, and it is probable that this city may be identified with Nineveh.[1] That in the time of Ḫammurabi the country to the north of Babylonia was known as

---

[1] Amiaud held that Ninâ, Girsu, Uru-azagga and Gishgalla, were not separate cities but districts of Shirpurla (see *Revue archéologique*, Juillet–Août, 1888, pp. 67 ff.). But Hommel's identification of Ninâ with Nineveh is very probable (see his *Geschichte*, p. 327 f., and cp. Jensen in Schrader's *Keilinschriftliche Bibliothek*, III, p. 5, note 1).

Assyria, and probably formed an integral part of
Hammurabi's dominions, was proved some six years
ago by a reference to the country found in one of
Hammurabi's letters to Sin-idinnam, governor of
Larsam, in which he directs him to despatch to him
" two hundred and forty men of the King's Company
" under the command of Nannar-iddina, who are of the
" force that is in thy hand and who have left the country
" of Ashur and the district of Shitullum." [1]

The conclusion drawn from this letter of Hammurabi
has met with striking confirmation in two phrases in the
introduction to the Code of Laws of Hammurabi engraved upon the great diorite stele which was found at
Susa by M. De Morgan. Here Hammurabi is described
as one " who hath restored his (i.e. Ashur's) protecting
" image unto the city of Ashur," [2] and a few lines further
on as " the king who hath made the names of Ishtar
" glorious in the city of Nineveh in the temple of
" E-mishmish." [3] From these passages it will be seen
that Hammurabi conferred benefits upon Ashur and
Nineveh, and speaks of both cities as though they lay
within the limits of his own empire.

---

[1] See my *Letters of Hammurabi*, Vol. I, p. xliii, pl. 37 (Brit. Mus.
No. 12,863) and Vol. III, pp. 3 ff.

[2] See *Délégation en Perse, Mémoires*, Tome IV, *Textes Élamites-
Sémitiques*, par V. Scheil, deux. sér., pl. 4, col. IV, ll. 55–58, *mu-te-iṣ
ilu lamassi-šu da-mi-iḳ-tim a-na alu Aššur KI*.

[3] *Cf. op. cit.*, col. IV, ll. 60–63, *šarru ša i-na Ni-nu-a KI i-na E-miš-miš
u-šu-bi-u me-e ilu Ištar.*

Until the publication of Hammurabi's letter referred to above, it had always been assumed that the earliest *patesi*, or "governors," of Assyria whose names were known to us were Ishme-Dagan and his son Shamshi-Adad, who, as was concluded from a reference to them on the cylinder of Tiglath-pileser I,[1] ruled a little before B.C. 1800. Other Assyrian *patesi* whose names, but not dates, were known, such as Shamshi-Adad,[2] the son of Igur-kapkapu, and Irishum,[3] the son of Khallu, had hitherto been placed at some period after Ishme-Dagan and Shamshi-Adad. But in view of the early reference to Assyria upon Hammurabi's letter I made the suggestion that it was possible that they ruled at a considerably earlier date than Ishme-Dagan.[4]

This suggestion with regard to Shamshi-Adad has now been confirmed by an interesting oath-formula found by Dr. Hermann Ranke on a contract-tablet of the reign of Hammurabi preserved in the Pennsylvania Museum. From this document it may legitimately be inferred that an Assyrian *patesi* of the name of

---

[1] See Budge and King, *Annals of the Kings of Assyria*, p. 95 f., col. VII, ll. 60 ff.

[2] *Op. cit.*, p. 2.

[3] *Op. cit.*, p. 1.

[4] See *Letters of Hammurabi*, Vol. III, p. 5. It is possible that Ikunum, another early Assyrian *patesi*, was the son of Irishum and the grandson of Khallu, for on an Assyrian copy of a votive inscription of his (K. 8805 + K. 10,238 + K. 10,880) he is styled the son of *Erishum*, which may be a variant form of the name of Irishum; see Johns, *Am. Journ. Sem. Lang.*, Vol. XVIII, p. 176.

Shamshi-Adad ruled in Assyria as a viceroy or
governor under Ḫammurabi,[1] and as Shamshi-Adad,
the son of Ishme-Dagan, lived too late to be identified
with him, we may provisionally assume that Ḫammurabi's viceroy was Shamshi-Adad, the son of Igur-
kapkapu. From the fact that his brick-inscription
in the British Museum does not apply the title of *patesi*
to his father, Igur-kapkapu, it may be inferred that he
did not inherit the throne of Assyria, but owed his
own appointment as *patesi* to Ḫammurabi.

In the centuries succeeding the period of the First
Dynasty we have little knowledge of the relations
which existed between Assyria and Babylonia, but
such indications as we possess point to the gradual
growth of Assyria in power until she ultimately
obtained her independence.[2] We may perhaps regard

---

[1] Dr. Ranke has not yet published the tablet in question, but he tells
me that the name Shamshi-Adad is associated with that of Ḫammurabi
in the oath-formula upon the tablet. As only the names of gods and
kings are mentioned in oath-formulae of the First Dynasty, it follows
that Shamshi-Adad was a king, or at any rate a *patesi*. Dr. Ranke, who
has made a special study of the proper names of this period, will point out
that from its form the name *Shamshi-Adad* can only be that of an
Assyrian, not of a Babylonian. It therefore follows that an Assyrian *patesi*
named Shamshi-Adad was a contemporary of Ḫammurabi, and, as he is
associated with him in the oath-formula, it may be concluded that he was not
an independent ruler, but governed Assyria as a dependency of Babylon.

[2] To this period of transition it is possible that we should assign
Bêl-kapkapi, an early Assyrian ruler, who, according to Adad-nirari III
(B.C. 812–B.C. 783), lived before Sululi, "whom Ashur duly called (to be
king) in days of old." See *Cun. Inscr. West. Asia*, Vol. I, pl. 35, No. 3,
ll. 23 ff.

Bêl-ibni as the first independent king of Assyria, inasmuch as Esarhaddon describes him as "the founder of the kingdom of Assyria,"[1] but the circumstances which led to the founding of the kingdom and the period at which the event took place are alike unknown. No doubt the pressure of the Kassite tribes, which was already beginning to be felt during the latter half of the First Dynasty,[2] considerably weakened Babylon and gave Assyria her opportunity.

As one of the results of her emancipation we know that at about 1500 B.C. the reigning Assyrian king sent gifts, as an independent ruler, to Thothmes III, king of Egypt. This took place in the twenty-fourth year of the reign of Thothmes, and in his fortieth year he records that he received another present from an Assyrian king.[3] In like manner at the end of the fifteenth century B.C. Ashûr-nadin-akhê, the father of Ashur-uballit, established friendly relations with the king of Egypt and exchanged gifts with him, and a similar friendship existed between Ashur-uballit, the son of Ashur-nadin-akhê, and Amen-hetep IV.[4] This

---

[1] See *Mittheilungen aus den Orientalischen Sammlungen*, Heft XI (*Sendschirli I*), Taf. V, ll. 17 ff.

[2] See my *Letters of Ḫammurabi*, Vol. III, pp. lxix, 233 f.

[3] See Lepsius, *Denkmäler*, Vol. III, p. 32, ll. 36, 32.

[4] These facts are known from one of the letters from Tell el-Amarna (now at Cairo), addressed to Amen-hetep IV by Ashur-uballit; see Winckler, *Thontafelfund von el Amarna*, p. 8, No. 9.

evidence is sufficient to prove that during the fifteenth century Assyria was a powerful and independent nation with a well-defined foreign policy.

At this point in her history the so-called "Synchronous History" of Assyria and Babylonia furnishes us with a series of brief notices concerning the relations which existed between the two countries, and from them we learn the sequence of events which culminated nearly two hundred years later in Tukulti-Ninib's conquest of Babylon. About B.C. 1450 Ashur-bêl-nishêshu, king of Assyria, and Kara-indash, king of Babylonia, made a friendly agreement with one another with regard to the boundary separating their two countries, and some twenty-five years later a similar agreement was entered into by Puzur-Ashur and Burnaburiash, the Babylonian king.[1] These friendly relations were continued by Ashur-uballiṭ (about B.C. 1400), who married his daughter Muballiṭat-Sherûa to Burnaburiash. On the death of Burnaburiash, Kara-khardash his son, who was the grandson of Ashur-uballiṭ, ascended the throne of Babylon, and it was probably due to his Assyrian sympathies that the Kassite party in Babylon revolted and slew him and set Nazibugash in his place. Ashur-uballiṭ invaded Babylonia, and having slain Nazibugash, put Kurigalzu

[1] See the "Synchronous History" (K. 4401a + R. 854), col. I, ll. 12–15 and ll. 16–18 ; cf. Winckler, *Untersuchungen*, p. 148.

the younger, another son of Burnaburiash, upon the throne.[1]

But Ashur-uballiṭ did not succeed in permanently restoring the intimate relations which had existed for so many years between Assyria and Babylonia, for under his son, Bêl-nirari, Kurigalzu led an expedition against Assyria. Kurigalzu's attempt to conquer Assyria was not successful, and after his defeat he was obliged to cede territory to Bêl-nirari. A further extension of Assyrian territory took place under Adad-nirari I, who defeated Nazi-marattash, the Babylonian king.[2] Thus it will be seen that at the

---

[1] See the "Synchronous History," col. I, ll. 19–28. The Babylonian Chronicle, 82–7–4, 38 (col. I) states that it was Kadashman-kharbe, the son of Kara-khardash, whom the Kassites slew, and it gives the name of the usurper as Shuzigash ; cf. Winckler, *Altorientalische Forschungen*, I, pp. 115 f., 298.

[2] *Op. cit.*, col. I, ll. 29–34 and ll. 35–42 (restored from K. 2106). With regard to Adad-nirari I's victory, Mr. Johns remarks in the article "Nineveh," *Encycl. Bibl.*, Vol. III, col. 3422 f., that "Shalmaneser I relates that his father Adad-nirari, after an expedition into Babylon, brought back the gods of Babylon, Merodach and Nebo, and built them temples." If this were so, it would mean that Adad-nirari I anticipated Tukulti-Ninib in the capture of the capital. Mr. Johns refers to *Cun. Inscr. West. Asia*, Vol. III, No. 12 in support of his statement, and he evidently supposes that the inscription there published (No. 56–9–9, 171) is a bowl-inscription of Shalmaneser I. But the characters in which it is written show that it belongs to the late Assyrian period, and the traces of the name in l. 1 are certainly not those of Shalmaneser, but are probably the beginning of the name of Sargon (B.C. 722–705), to whom Sir Henry Rawlinson provisionally assigned the text. Moreover, the inscription makes no reference to an expedition into Babylon, but merely records the restoration of a temple dedicated to Nabû and Marduk, which had been previously restored by Adad-nirari (probably Adad-nirari III).

end of the fourteenth century two Assyrian kings, one of them the grandfather of Tukulti-Ninib I, had defeated Babylonian armies, and had exacted cessions of Babylonian territory as the result of their victories. Tukulti-Ninib I was only following in their steps when he defeated Bibeashu. His achievement, however, differs from those of his predecessors in degree, for he succeeded in capturing Babylon itself and in deporting the Babylonian king, and, instead of merely acquiring a fresh strip of Babylonian territory, he subdued the whole country and administered it as a province of his empire until his death.

In addition to the information concerning Tukulti-Ninib's reign afforded by his memorial tablet and by the Chronicle 83-7-4, 38, we also know from inscribed bricks found at Kuyunjik that he restored the great temple of Ishtar at Nineveh.[1] The only other inscription of Tukulti-Ninib I which has been recovered up to the present time is his well-known seal-inscription, which was engraved upon a seal of lapis-lazuli, and is now extant in a copy on a clay tablet made by a scribe of Sennacherib. This tablet, by means of which the date of Tukulti-Ninib can be approximately fixed, is numbered K. 2673, and it is

---

[1] One of Tukulti-Ninib's brick-inscriptions reads: (1) *ᵐTukulti(ti)-ⁱˡᵘNin-ib* (2) *šar kiššati apil ⁱˡᵘŠulmânu-ašaridu* (3) *šar kiššati ba-ni bît* *ⁱˡᵘIštar* (4) *ša ᵃˡᵘNi-nu-a*, "Tukulti-Ninib, king of hosts, son of Shalmaneser, king of hosts, builder of the temple of Ishtar of Nineveh." For a variant inscription, see George Smith, *Assyr. Disc.*, p. 249.

Obverse.

Edge.

Reverse.

Seal-inscriptions of Shagarakti-Shuriash and Tukulti-Ninib I, inscribed
upon a clay tablet of the time of Sennacherib [K. 2673].

published and translated in the present volume under the Supplementary Texts.

The tablet is inscribed with a rough draft of the lines which Sennacherib desired to be added to the inscription already engraved upon the seal, in commemoration of its recovery by himself on the occasion of his conquest of Babylon. On the reverse of the tablet is a copy of the text which Sennacherib found upon the seal ; on the obverse and edge a copy of the original text is repeated, together with the additional lines which Sennacherib proposed to have inscribed. The meaning of the phrase *gar-ri ik-ta-din*, which occurs in the first line of Sennacherib's addition, is not certain. If, as is suggested in the translation of the text given below,[1] the words may be rendered "the enemy carried away," it follows that Tukulti-Ninib's seal was removed from Assyria to Babylon either at the time of the successful revolt headed by Adad-shum-uṣur, or at some subsequent period,[2] and was recaptured by Sennacherib on his conquest of Babylon "after six hundred years." The phrase "after six hundred years" is usually taken to refer to the interval between Tukulti-Ninib's date and the capture of Babylon by Sennacherib ; but it may equally well

---

[1] See the Supplementary Texts, p. 107.

[2] Possibly by Tukulti-Ashur, in whose time Marduk's statue, which had been removed to Assyria by Tukulti-Ninib I, was restored to Babylon see below p. 72.

apply to the date of the removal of the seal from
Assyria, which may possibly have taken place some
years after Tukulti-Ninib's death.

Another element of uncertainty which enters into the
problem is due to the fact that Sennacherib conquered
Babylon twice, the first time in 702 B.C., and again in
689 B.C. On the first occasion he states that he entered
Merodach-baladan's palace in Babylon with joy, and
opened his treasure-house, and carried away the
treasures it contained,[1] and Tukulti-Ninib's seal may
well have been among the objects he then removed.
But on the second occasion, in 689 B.C., Sennacherib
records that he not only despoiled Babylon of her
costly treasures, but recovered two images, of Adad
and Shala, which Marduk-nadin-akhê had carried
away to Babylon in the time of Tiglath-pileser I.[2]
It may with some probability be urged that the seal
of Tukulti-Ninib was recovered at the same time that
the statues of Adad and Shala were brought back, for
both the seal and the statues were trophies of victories
over Assyria, and may well have been preserved in the
same building.

But the question whether the seal was recovered in

---

[1] See the Supplementary Texts, where a translation is given of the
extract from Sennacherib's prism, which records this first conquest of
Babylon.

[2] A portion of the Bavian inscription refers to this second conquest of
Babylon, and a translation of the extract, from my own edition of the texts,
is given below in the Supplementary Texts.

702 B.C. or in 689 B.C. is not of very great importance, for it is obvious that Sennacherib in mentioning six hundred years is speaking in round numbers. To accept the six hundred years as mathematically accurate to a day, and to assert on this evidence that Tukulti-Ninib I was reigning in 1302 B.C. or in 1289 B.C., is to force too rigid a meaning into Sennacherib's words. They can only be legitimately held to prove that in the time of Sennacherib it was believed that Tukulti-Ninib's reign might be approximately referred to the beginning, or the early part, of the thirteenth century. His reign may be provisionally placed at about 1275 B.C.

The tablet inscribed with Sennacherib's copy oi Tukulti-Ninib's seal contains a line of text, partly written in archaic characters and repeated on the reverse of the tablet, which has always proved puzzling, and has not hitherto been satisfactorily explained. The late Mr. George Smith in his translation of the text[1] did not attempt a rendering of it, neither did Prof. Hommel,[2] nor Prof. Bezold,[3] nor Prof. Schrader,[4] in the renderings they have published. Prof. Sayce took the

---

[1] See *Trans. Soc. Bibl. Arch.*, Vol. I, p. 71, and *Records of the Past*, Vol. V, p. 85 f.

[2] In his *Geschichte Babyloniens und Assyriens*, p. 439, note 1.

[3] See his *Babylonisch-Assyrische Literatur*, p. 15 f.

[4] Prof. Schrader remarks: "Z. 8, am Rand stehend, mir unverständlich;" see *Keilinschriftliche Bibliothek*, I, p. 10.

f

line to be the concluding part of the seal-inscription of
Tukulti-Ninib, and rendered it as a complete sentence
with a relative clause.[1]

In the *Annals of the Kings of Assyria* the possibility
is suggested that the line "was not part of Tukulti-
"Ninib's inscription, but was engraved upon the seal
"by its first owner before Tukulti-Ninib captured it in
"Babylon."[2] At the time that was written I recognized
that the line contained a proper name, but I had not
succeeded in making it out. Now, however, I think it
can be shown that the line contains the name and title
of Shagarakti-Shuriash, the former owner of the seal,
who immediately preceded Bibeashu upon the throne of
Babylon, and was living within nine years of Tukulti-
Ninib's capture of the city.[3] On p. 69 I have given a
conjectural restoration of the original Old-Babylonian
inscription which was engraved upon the seal of lapis-

---

[1] Prof. Sayce translated the line as "Whoever makes the seal legible (?)
"[ensures?] the preservation of my life"; see *Records of the Past*, New
Series, Vol. V, p. ix, note 1.

[2] See *Annals of the Kings of Assyria*, p. 15, note 2.

[3] Thus it will be seen that the seal was not made originally for Tukulti-
Ninib I, but for the Kassite king, Shagarakti-Shuriash. Tukulti-Ninib
found the seal in Babylon, on his capture of the city, and had his own
inscription engraved upon it without erasing that of Shagarakti-Shuriash.
Tukulti-Ninib carried the seal to Assyria, but it was afterwards removed to
Babylon. Sennacherib when he captured Babylon (either in 702 B.C. or
in 689 B.C.) found the seal, and on the clay tablet K. 2673 his scribe wrote
out copies of the original texts upon the seal and a draft of Sennacherib's
proposed addition to them.

lazuli. Under it is the copy made by the Assyrian scribe of the time of Sennacherib upon the clay tablet K. 2673. On the plate I have numbered the twelve signs of the inscription, and have placed under them the values which should be assigned to them. I think that a single glance at the plate will suffice to show that the conjectural restoration of the original text is correct.

It should be noted that the scribe himself did not recognize many of the characters upon the seal. This is clear from an examination of his copy of Tukulti-Ninib's inscription. As this was written in archaic Assyrian characters, and not in archaic Babylonian characters, he could read the greater part of it, and he has therefore turned it into modern Assyrian characters. But the verb in l. 2 he did not understand, so in the case of this word he has copied the archaic forms of the characters as he saw them.[1] Similarly in the lines under discussion he was certain of the signs TI and IA, and he has therefore given them their modern Assyrian forms. But the other signs he failed to make out, and so he gave a copy of what he saw upon the stone. It will be observed that his copy is fairly accurate, and that he has reproduced the essential form of each of the signs.

---

[1] This verb he has copied as *mu-kak-kir*; but the sign he has taken for ⟨sign⟩ was really ⟨sign⟩, and the verb was *mu-ni-kir*. This is the usual form of the Participle of the Piel of *nakâru* during the early Assyrian period, as *u-ni-kir* was the form of the Pret. Piel of the same verb (see the Appendix).

f 2

Taking the twelve characters in the line in the order in which they occur, we may note how far the scribe has copied them correctly. No. 1 is clearly the character 𒌋; the scribe has omitted the small wedge in the centre, possibly because it was rubbed on the seal, or he may have taken the original for an archaic Assyrian 𒌋. Signs 2 and 3 he has copied fairly accurately, except that he has omitted the three small upright lines from the centre of GA (No. 2); this sign occurs again as No. 4, and he has made the same omission in his copy. No. 5, which is really RA (𒊏), he has copied as ŠA (𒊭), possibly thinking that the groups Nos. 2 and 3 and Nos. 4 and 5 were the same sign repeated (*i.e.*, the group DUB-DUB, Br. No. 7037). No. 6, the sign AK, is correct, except that he has written too few horizontal wedges; that he was uncertain how many wedges the original contained is clear from the fact that in the copy on the reverse he has written an extra wedge. No. 7 is correct, and he has turned it into its Assyrian form.

Sign No. 8, the Old-Babylonian form of 𒌋, has evidently puzzled the scribe. He has seen that it began with a horizontal wedge, and that it had two vertical wedges in the upper part; but the three lower wedges, all pointing different ways, were too much for him; so he has compromised the matter by writing two diagonal wedges. No. 9 is correct, and, like No. 7, he has turned it into its modern Assyrian form. No. 10 is correct. No. 11, the sign for "king," is nearly correct, for he has

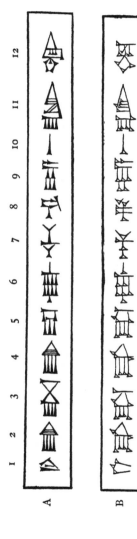

	1	2	3	4	5	6	7	8	9	10	11	12

ŠA - GA ŠA - GA - RA - AK - TI - ŠUR - IA - AŠ LUGAL KIŠ
(*makkur*) (*šar*) (*kiššati*)

Inscription of Shagarakti-Shuriash, king of Babylon, engraved upon a seal of lapis-lazuli, on which inscriptions were afterwards added by Tukulti-Ninib I and Sennacherib.

A. Conjectural restoration of the original inscription engraved upon the seal.

B. Copy of the inscription made upon the clay tablet K. 2673 by the order of Sennacherib.

only omitted the two slight diagonal lines in the centre
of the character. No. 12, the last sign in the line, is a
good copy as to its general form, but the pointed end
of the original character he has taken for the ends of
two wedges crossing one another and projecting from
the inside of the sign. Thus it will be seen that in only
one case (No. 5) has he definitely misread a character,
and this he has done by adding a single wedge, and
slightly altering the direction of two others.

The original text upon the seal, restored as indicated
on p. 69, and written in modern Assyrian characters,
reads : 𒀭 ... , *makkur Ša-ga-ra-ak-ti-Šur-ia-aš šar kiššati,*[1]
"Property of Shagarakti-Shuriash, king of hosts." It
may be added that this reading of the name upon the
seal proves that the king's name in question is to be
read *Shagarakti-Shuriash*, and not *Shagashalti-Shuriash*,
as it is often read at present.[2]

Though by means of Sennacherib's addition to
Tukulti-Ninib's seal-inscription we are enabled to fix
approximately the date at which he lived, we have no
means of determining the length of his reign. From the
Chronicle, 82–7–4, 38, we know that he was slain in a

---

[1] The sign ⟨⟨⟨ , in the title ... ⟨⟨⟨ , must be read at this period
as *kiššati*, not as the name of the city of Kish.

[2] Elsewhere the third syllable of the name is written ... , which has
both the values *šal* and *rak* ; in K. 2673 the syllable is written ... ,
ra-ak, proving that the latter is the correct reading.

revolt headed by his son Ashur-naṣir-pal, who succeeded him upon the throne. This is the only information we possess of the reign of Ashur-naṣir-pal I, but we may perhaps infer from l. 12 of the Chronicle, that his successor was Tukulti-Ashur,[1] in whose time the statue of Marduk, which Tukulti-Ninib had carried to Assyria, was restored to Babylon. Two other Assyrian kings may perhaps be added to the list of Tukulti-Ninib's immediate successors, *i.e.*, Ashur-narara and Nabû-dâni. The names of these two kings occur on a late Assyrian copy of an Old-Babylonian letter [2] addressed to them by a Babylonian king named Adad-shum-naṣir.[3]   It is

---

[1] Mr. Pinches, Prof. Sayce, and Dr. Winckler have read this name as Tukulti-Ashur-Bêl (see *Records of the Past*, New Series, Vol. V, p. 111, and *Altorientalischer Forschungen*, I, pp. 124, 136), and they have been followed by Prof. Rogers in his *History of Babylonia and Assyria*, Vol. II, p. 17. But Bêl is not part of the proper name, but is the subject of the sentences in the Chronicle in which the name occurs. Dr. Winckler translates the passage as : "sechs jahre bis auf Tukultu-Aššur-Bîl in Assyrien "sass er. zur zeit Tukulti-Aššur-Bîl's nach Babylon kam er," and in a footnote to " er " he asks "wer ? ". Of course Bêl is the subject of the two verbs, and the meaning is that Bêl's statue (*i.e.*, the statue of Marduk), which had been carried away from Babylon by Tukulti-Ninib, remained in Assyria until the time of Tukulti-Ashur, when it was restored to Babylon ; see the translation of the passage in the Supplementary Texts.

[2] The Assyrian copy, which was found at Kuyunjik, is numbered K. 3045, and has been published in *Cun. Inscr. West. Asia*, Vol. III, pl. 4, No. 5. K. 2641 is a fragment of another Assyrian copy of an Old-Babylonian letter, addressed by a king of Assyria to his father, the king of Babylon. This letter, like K. 3045, may probably be assigned to the period of the Third Dynasty.

[3] The name is written on the letter as *m ilu*Adad-*šum*-šeš-*ir*, i.e., *Adad-šum-naṣir(ir)*, for the reading *Adad-mu-šeš-ir*, i.e., Adad-mušêšir (see

possible that this king is to be identified with Adad-shum-uṣur of the Babylonian List of Kings and of the Chronicle, 82–7–4, 38. In that case both the names should be read as Adad-shum-naṣir, or as Adad-shum-uṣur, and it would follow that Ashur-narara and Nabû-dâni reigned soon after Tukulti-Ninib.

There is a difficulty with regard to Tukulti-Ninib's seven years' rule in Babylon, for his name is not mentioned in the Babylonian List of Kings. According to this document three kings reigned between Bibe and Adad-shum-uṣur, the passage in the List (obv. col. II, ll. 6–11),[1] which refers to this period and gives the names of the kings with the lengths of their reigns, reading :—

13 years	Shagarak[ti-Shuria]sh.
8 years	Bibe, his son.
1 year and 6 months	Bêl-nadin-shum.
1 year and 6 months	Kadashman-kharbi.
6 years	Adad-shum-iddina.
30 years	Adad-shum-uṣur.

Hilprecht, *Old Bab. Inscr. chiefly from Nippur*, p. 34), is improbable. The name of the king usually read as Adad-shum-uṣur is written *m ilu Adad-šum*-šEš, which may also be read as Adad-šum-naṣir. Winckler suggests that the syllable *ir* in the letter K. 3045 may be due to an error of the copyist, in which case both names would be read as Adad-šum-uṣur (see *Altorientalische Forschungen*, I, p. 124, note 3).

[1] See Winckler, *Untersuchungen*, p. 146.

From the above extract it will be seen that the reigns of Bêl-nadin-shum, Kadashman-kharbi, and Adad-shum-iddina occupied altogether nine years. According to the Chronicle, 82–7–4, 38, between Bibeiashu and Adad-shum-uṣur came the seven years of Tukulti-Ninib's rule in Babylon. Moreover, in the Chronicle the reigns of Bêl-nadin-shum and Adad-shum-iddina occur after Adad-shum-uṣur, and not before him as in the Kings' List.

Prof. Hommel seeks to explain this discrepancy by identifying the period of Tukulti-Ninib's reign in Babylon (7 years) with the period of the reigns of Bêl-nadin-shum, Kadashman-kharbi, and Adad-shum-iddina (9 years), and he suggests that these three rulers either were opponents who rose against Tukulti-Ninib and were defeated by him, or were vassal kings who ruled under him. In order to fit this theory in, he has to assume that the order of the separate sections in col. IV of the Chronicle, 82–7–4, 38, is not chronological, and that the second and third sections are added to the first by way of appendices. Also, he assumes that Adad-shum-uṣur was the son of Adad-shum-iddina and not of Tukulti-Ninib I, and that when the Chronicle (col. IV, 1. 9) says that the nobles of Akkad and Karduniash set Adad-shum-uṣur on his father's throne, the reference is to his succeeding Adad-shum-iddina, not Tukulti-Ninib.[1]

---

[1] See Hommel in Winckler's *Altorientalische Forschungen*, I, p. 138 f. Dr. Winckler adopts Prof. Hommel's theory.

But the difficulties of this reconciliation of the two documents are almost greater than the discrepancies which it sets out to explain away. For there is no other instance in the Babylonian Chronicle of the separate sections occurring out of chronological order, and if the compiler of the Chronicle knew that Tukulti-Ninib I defeated Bêl-nadin-shum, Kadashman-kharbi, and Adad-shum-iddina, or appointed them as vassal kings, and if he knew that their reigns occurred before that of Adad-shum-uṣur, there is absolutely no reason why he should not have said so and have given their reigns in the proper order. It is easier to suppose that the discrepancies between the Kings' List and the Chronicle are real discrepancies, resulting from two different traditions with regard to the order of the kings of this part of the Third Dynasty; and as a similar instance of a variant tradition preserved by the Chronicle, 82-7-4, 38, we may compare the account it gives of Ashur-uballiṭ's intervention in Babylonian affairs with the corresponding narrative in the "Synchronous History."[1]

We are thus in the position of having two variant accounts to choose from, both coming to us upon tablets of the late Babylonian period, and referring to events which took place many centuries before the time at which the texts upon them were compiled.

---

[1] See above, page 59, note 1.

Instead of exercising our ingenuity in attempts at reconciling the two accounts, it is preferable to recognize the existence of two variant traditions, and to await the discovery of some contemporary document, such as the memorial tablet of Tukulti-Ninib I, which will offer unimpeachable evidence with regard to the correct sequence of the Babylonian kings of the period.

In the following pages the text of the annals of Tukulti-Ninib is given from his memorial tablet together with a translation and a transliteration. This is succeeded by a series of supplementary inscriptions, consisting of the texts and extracts referred to in the course of this introduction as throwing light upon Tukulti-Ninib's date and the period of his rule in Babylon.

TEXTS AND TRANSLATIONS.

I.

THE ANNALS OF TUKULTI-NINIB I.

Obv.

1. [cuneiform text]¹

2. [cuneiform text]²

3. [cuneiform text]

4. [cuneiform text]³

5. [cuneiform text]

---

¹ So the traces at the end of the line are probably to be restored. The whole of l. 1 is much rubbed or weather-worn, but the traces of all the signs, with the exception of the last three, are quite clear.

² The reading of [sign] between [sign] and [sign] is certain; the signs are cut very close together and partly covered by silicate. The scribe probably omitted [sign] and then wrote it in, one of its wedges partly covering the beginning of [sign].

TRANSLATION.

1. Tukulti-Ninib, the king of hosts, the king of Assyria, the king of the four quarters[1] (of the world),
2. the mighty king, the king of Karduniash,[2] the king of Sumer and Akkad,
3. the king of the Upper and the Lower Sea, the king of the highlands
4. and of the broad plains,[3] the king of the Shubarî and the Ḳutî, and the king of all
5. the lands of Na'iri, the king whom the gods have caused to attain unto the triumph of his heart's desire,

TRANSLITERATION.

1. ᵐ Tukulti(ti)- ⁱˡᵘNin-ib šar kiššati šar ᵐᵃᵗᵘ ⁱˡᵘA-šur šar kib-r[at irbitti(ti)] ¹
2. šarru dan-nu šar ᵐᵃᵗᵘ ² Kar-du-ni-aš šar ᵐᵃᵗᵘ Šu-me-ri u Ak-ka-di-i
3. šar tâmdi e-li-ti u šu-pa-li-ti šar ḫur-ša-ni
4. u na-me-e ³ rapšûti ᵖˡ šar ᵐᵃᵗᵘ Šu-ba-ri-i Ḳu-ti-i u šar kul-la-at
5. mâtâti Na-'i-ri šarru ša ir-nin-tu lib-bi-šu ilâni ᵖˡ

³ To namû, pl. namê, which usually has the meaning "ruins," must here be assigned some such meaning as "plains." This is proved both by its use in antithesis to ḫursâni and by the adjective rapšûti. The connection of this meaning with an original root namû, "to fall, to sink, to lie prone," is obvious.

Obv.

6. 𒄑𒌷𒈦 𒂊𒇺 𒀭𒁀 𒀀𒈨 𒂊 𒂊 𒁀𒁹 𒀜
   𒆠 𒂊𒌷 𒆸 𒀀𒁹 𒁹 𒌋 [1]

7. 𒈛 𒂊 𒀀𒆜 𒂊 [2] 𒈠 𒂍 𒆤𒆠 𒄑𒌷𒈦
   𒁹 𒀀𒁹 𒁁

8. 𒁹 𒀜 𒈨𒅎 𒂊 𒁁 𒅆𒀀 𒌋𒌋 𒌍 𒌋𒌋
   𒐊 𒀜 𒁹 𒇬 𒁹 𒃻 𒆤𒉌 𒌋𒌋 𒌍
   𒌋𒌋 𒐊 𒀜 𒁹 𒇬 𒂊

9. 𒆠 𒀀𒁹   𒇬 𒀸𒈬   𒌋𒌋 𒀀𒆜 𒈨𒁹
   𒆠 𒀀𒁹 𒂊𒇺 𒀜𒋢 𒆠   𒀀𒆜 𒈨𒁹
   𒐊 𒆸𒈨 𒀀𒆜 𒆠

10. 𒐊 𒄑𒌷𒈦 𒆸𒈨𒂊 𒈠 𒆠 𒐊 𒐖𒈨 𒀀𒈬 𒈠 𒁹
    𒀭𒂍 𒐊 𒂍𒁁 𒈠 𒂊𒁹

11. 𒐊 𒁹 𒀀𒈨 𒀜𒋢 𒁹𒁹 𒀀𒆜 𒂍
    𒀜𒋢 𒃻𒈨 𒃰𒅎 𒐊 𒐊 𒂊 𒀭

12. 𒀭𒂍 𒀀 𒂊𒁹 𒇷 𒀀𒈠 𒌋 𒈠 𒂊 𒀭
    𒃻 𒆸𒈨 𒂊

13. 𒆠 𒀀𒁹 𒀜𒁹 𒂊𒁹 𒀜 𒁹 𒀸𒈬 𒂍
    𒃻 𒂊𒁹 𒐊𒐊 𒀭𒀜𒁹𒋢

OBV.

6. so that with the staff[1]
7. of his might he hath shepherded the four quarters (of the world), am I ;
8. the son of Shalmaneser, the king of hosts, the king of Assyria, the son of Adad-nirari, the king of hosts, the king of Assyria.
9. In the beginning of my sovereignty, in the first year of my reign, the Kutî
10. and the Uḳumanî and the lands of Elkhunia and Sharnida
11. and Mekhri my hand conquered, and the tribute of their mountains
12. and the wealth of their highlands every year
13. in my city of Ashur I received.

OBV.

6. *u-šiḳ-ši-du-šu-ma kib-rat irbitta(ta) i-na šib-baṭ* [1]
7. *kiš-šu-ti-šu[2] ir-te-'u-u a-na-ku*
8. *apil ᶦˡᵘŠulmânu(nu)-ašaridu šar kiššati šar ᵐᵃᵗᵘ ᶦˡᵘA-šur apil Adad-nirari šar kiššati šar ᵐᵃᵗᵘ ᶦˡᵘA-šur-ma*
9. *i-na šur-ru šarru-ti-ia i-na maḫ-ri-i palî-ia ᵐᵃᵗᵘKu-ti-i*
10. *ᵐᵃᵗᵘU-ḳu-ma-ni-i ᵐᵃᵗᵘEl-ḫu-ni-a u ᵐᵃᵗᵘŠar-ni-da*
11. *ᵐᵃᵗᵘMe-iḫ-ri ḳa-a-ti lu ik-šud bilat šadâni-šu-nu*
12. *u ḫi-ṣi-ib ḫur-ša-ni-šu-nu šatti-šam-ma*
13. *i-na ali-ia ᶦˡᵘA-šur lu am-da-ḫa-ar*

---

[1] The rendering *šib-baṭ kiš-šu-ti-šu*, "the staff of his might," is more probable than *šib-be*, "girdle," or *šib-baṭ*, "flame," from the root *šabâbu* ; *šib-baṭ* is probably the construct of a form *šibbaṭu*, and is not to be taken as *šibaṭ*, a construct of *šibṭu*.

[2] The signs ⪤ and ⪥ are engraved over an erasure.

g

Obv.

14. 𒐏 [cuneiform signs]

15. [cuneiform signs]

16. [cuneiform signs]

17. [cuneiform signs]¹

18. [cuneiform signs]² [cuneiform signs] [cuneiform signs]³

19. [cuneiform signs]

20. [cuneiform signs]

---

¹ It is probable that *rappu* has some such meaning as "flame." For this meaning of the word, see the prism-inscription of Sennacherib, Col. I, l. 8, where the king is described as *rap-pu la-'i-it la ma-gi-ri*, "the *rappu* which burns up the disobedient." (*Cun. Inscr. of West. Asia*, Vol. I, pl. 37, l. 8.) Here [cuneiform signs] has hitherto been rendered as *rab-bu*, "the great one," but it should clearly be transliterated *rap-pu*, and the same meaning is to be assigned to it as in the present passage.

OBV.

14. At that time the Ḳurṭî, and the lands of Ḳummukhi, and Pushshe,
15. aṇd Mumme, and Alzi, and Madani, and Nikhani, and Alaia,
16. and Tearzi, and Purukuzzi, and the broad extent of the land of Shubarî
17. with flame[1] I burned, and the kings, their rulers,
18. I cast down[3] under my feet and ... I subjugated them.
19. Highlands and valleys, places that were impassable, whose paths no king
20. hath known, with the power of my abounding strength

OBV.

14. *i-na u-mi-šu-ma* ^{mâtu}*Ḳur-ṭi-i* ^{mâtu}*Ḳum-mu-ḫi* ^{mâtu}*Pu-uš-še*
15. ^{mâtu}*Mu-um-me* ^{mâtu}*Al-zi* ^{mâtu}*Ma-da-ni* ^{mâtu}*Ni-ḫa-ni* ^{mâtu}*A-la-ia*
16. ^{mâtu}*Te-ar-zi* ^{mâtu}*Pu-ru-kuz-zi u si-ḫir-ti* ^{mâtu}*Šu-ba-ri-i*
17. *rapašta(ta) i-na ra-ap-pi* [1] *lu-la-iṭ šarrâni^{pl} ša-pi-ri-šu-nu*
18. *a-na šêpê^{pl}-ia* [2] *u-šik-[ni]-iš* [3] *lu um-ši-ka e-mi-id*
19. *ḫur-ša-ni be-ru-ti a-šar la me-te-ḳi ša šarru ia-um-ma*
20. *ar-ḫa-te-šu-nu la i-du-u i-na li-it kiš-šu-ti-ia*

---

[2] The signs 𒐊 and 𒂊 are written over an erasure.
[3] If the text is correct as it stands, we must read *u-šig-iš*, II 1, Pret. from *šagâšu*," I destroyed." But, in view of the preceding phrase *a-na šêpê^{pl}-ia*, it is preferable to assume that the scribe has left out the sign 𒂊 by mistake and has not detected his omission ; *cf.* the erasures and corrections in ll. 2, 7, 18, 29, etc.

OBV.

21.

22.

23.

24.

25.

26.

27.

28.

29.

Obv.

21. I traversed, and forty[1] kings of the lands of Na'iri
22. to wage war and battle set themselves in mighty array.
23. I fought with them,
24. and I defeated them, and with their blood
25. I flooded the ravines and gullies of the mountains.
26. All their mountains I conquered, and toll and tribute
27. I laid upon them for ever.
28. With the help of Ashur, Bêl, and Shamash, the great gods,
29. my lords, and with the aid of Ishtar, the queen of heaven and earth,—

Obv.

21. *šu-tur-ti i-te-ik-ma arbâ(a)[1] ṣarrâni^{pl} mâtâti Na-'i-ri*
22. *a-na ka-ab-li u ta-ḫa-zi dap-ni-iš*
23. *iz-zi-zu-u-ni it-ti-šu-nu am-da-ḫa-aṣ*
24. *a-bi-ik-ta-šu-nu aš-ku-un dâmê^{pl}-šu-nu*
25. *ḫur-ri u muš-pa-li ša šadî(i) lu-me-ki-ir*
26. *kul-la-at šadâni-šu-nu a-bil bilta u ta-mar-ta*
27. *a-na u-um ṣa-a-ti eli-šu-nu aš-ku-un*
28. *i-na tukulti(ti) ša ^{ilu}A-šur ^{ilu}Bêl u ^{ilu}Ša-maš ilâni^{pl} rabûti^{pl}*
29. *bêlê^{pl}-ia ina ri[2]-ṣu-ti ša ^{ilu}Ištar rubât(at) šamê irṣiti(ti)*

---

[1] The sign 𒌋 is probably to be taken as the phonetic complement, and not as part of the numeral, 43.

[2] The signs ⊢ and ⊢𒅍 are written over an erasure.

OBV.

30. [cuneiform signs]

31. [cuneiform signs]

32. [cuneiform signs]

33. [cuneiform signs]

34. [cuneiform signs]

35. [cuneiform signs]

36. [cuneiform signs]

37. [cuneiform signs]

---

[1] It may perhaps be concluded from the context that *gal-tap-pi* has some such meaning as "refuse, mire." With the phrase we may compare the obscure similes used by Tiglath-pileser I in his great Cylinder-inscription. He there frequently states that he has scattered his enemies *ki-ma šut-ma-ši* (var. *še*), which may perhaps be rendered "like chaff" (Col. II, l. 14, Col. III, l. 79, Col. IV, l. 93; see Budge and King, *Annals of the Kings of Assyria*, Vol. I, pp. 39, 56, 68); or, he beats them down *ki-ma šu(-u)-be*, "like standing corn (?)" (Col. II, ll. 20, 80, Col. V, l. 94, Col.

OBV.

30. at the head of my warriors they (*i.e.*, the gods) marched, and Bibeashu,

31. king of Karduniash, I hemmed in to force him to wage battle.

32, I defeated his warriors, and his fighting men I brought low.

33. In the midst of that battle Bibeashu, king of the Kassites,

34. my hand captured, and his lordly neck like refuse [1]

35. I trampled under my feet, and as a captive and in fetters into the presence of Ashur,

36. my lord, I brought him. The whole of the lands of Sumer and Akkad

37. I conquered and unto the Lower Sea

OBV.

30. *ina pa-ni ṣâbê^{pl}-ia il-li-ku it-ti ^{m}Bi-be-a-šu*

31. *šar ^{mâtu}Kar-du-ni-aš ana e-piš tukmati(ti) as-ni-ik*

32. *a-bi-ik-ti ṣâbê^{pl}-šu aš-ku-un muk-tab-li-šu u-še-im-ḳit*

33. *ina ki-rib tam-ḥa-ri ša-a-tu ^{m}Bi-be-a-šu šar Kaš-ši-i*

34. *ḳa-a-ti ik-šud kišad be-lu-ti-šu ki-ma gal-tap-pi[1]*

35. *ina šêpê^{pl}-ia ak-bu-us šal²-lu-su ka-mu-su ana ma-ḥar ^{ilu}A-šur*

36. *bêli-ia u-bi-la ^{mâtu}Šu-me-ri u[3] Ak-ka-di-i*

37. *ana paṭ gim-ri-ša a-bil ana[4] tâmdi šu-pa-li-ti*

VI, l. 5, *Annals*, pp. 40, 46, 77, 78); or, he cuts off their heads *ki-ma zi-ir-ḳi*, "like swathes (?)" (Col. VI, l. 6, *Annals*, p. 79; *cf*. also Col. III, l. 98, *Annals*, p. 58).

[2] The signs ⵎ⟩ ⵎ⟩⟩⟨⟩ and ⟩ⵎ are written over an erasure.

[3] Written over an erasure.

[4] ⟩ seems to have been cut over the sign ⟩-, which the engraver had first cut by mistake.

Rev.

1.  𒀭 𒂊𒅀 𒂊 𒀀 𒂊𒅅𒌍 𒀀 𒀭 𒀀𒌍

2. 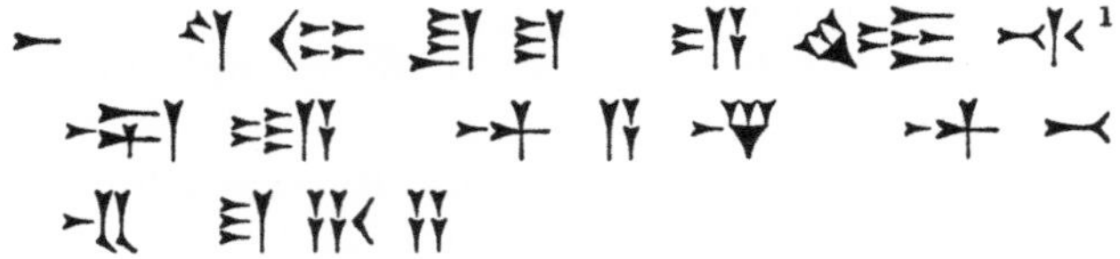 𒀀 𒁉 𒂊𒅀 𒂊𒅀 𒂊𒅀 𒅗𒀀 𒀀[1]
   𒀀 𒂊𒅀 𒀀 𒀀 𒀀 𒀀 𒀀
   𒀀 𒂊 𒅀 𒅀

3. 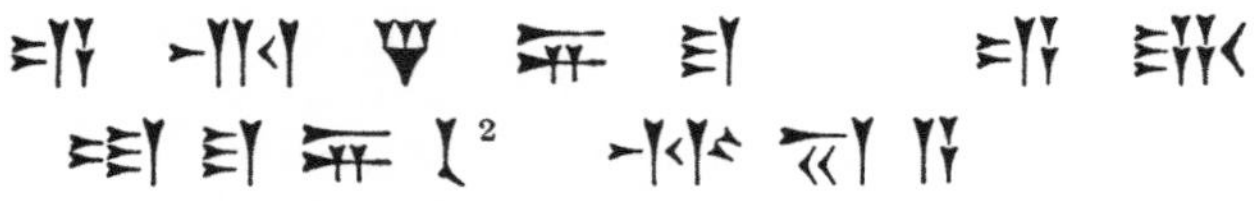 𒂊𒅀 𒀀 𒀭 𒀀 𒂊𒅀 𒂊𒅀 𒂊𒅀
   𒂊𒅀 𒂊𒅀 𒀀 𒀀[2] 𒀀 𒀀 𒅀

4.  𒀀 𒂊𒅀 𒂊𒅀° 𒀀 𒀀 𒀀 𒀀
   𒂊𒅀 𒅀 𒅀 𒂊𒅀 𒂊𒅀 𒀀 𒀀 𒂊𒅀

5. 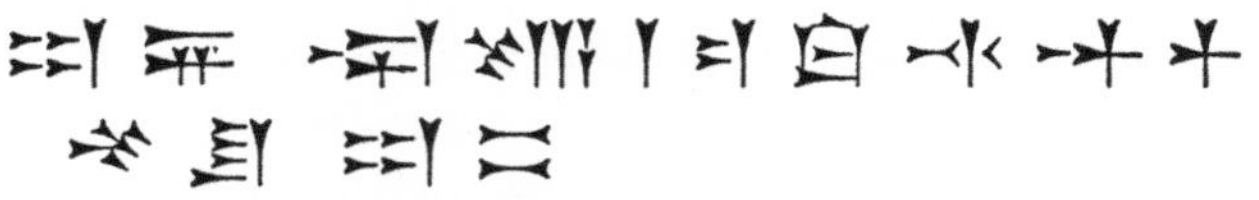 𒂊𒅀 𒀀 𒀀 � � 𒂊𒅀 𒀀 𒀀 �
   𒀀 𒂊𒅀 𒂊𒅀

6. 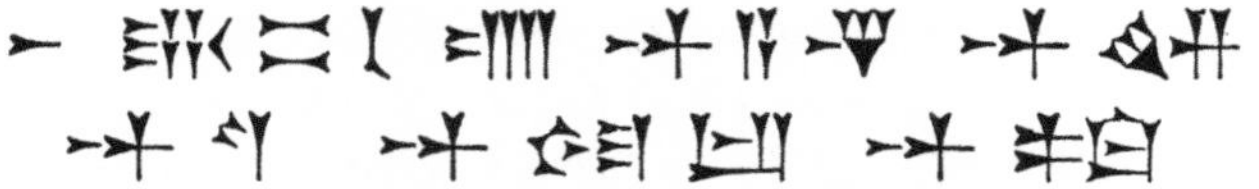 𒀀 𒂊𒅀 � 𒂊𒅀 𒀀 𒅀 𒀭 𒀀 𒀀
   𒀀 𒀀 𒀀 𒀀 𒀀 𒀀

7. 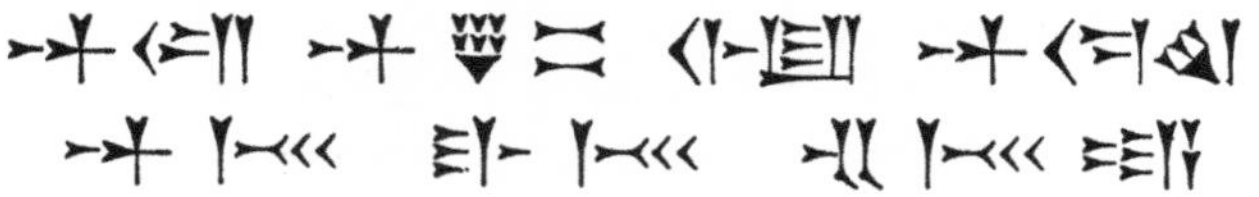 𒀀 𒂊𒅀 𒀀 𒀀 � � � � �
   � � 𒂊𒅀 � � � 𒂊𒅀

8.  𒂊𒅀 𒂊𒅀 𒂊𒅀 𒀀 𒂊𒅀 𒀀
   � 𒀭 𒀀 𒅀 � 𒂊𒅀 � � �

---

[1] The word *ebirtu* is used elsewhere of the further side of a river.

Rev.
1. of the Rising of the Sun I established the frontier of my land.
2. At that time beyond[1] my city of Ashur the lord Bêl commanded
3. that I should found a city and build a dwelling-place for him.
4. In accordance with[3] the desire of the gods a great city for my royal dwelling-place
5. I built, and Kar-Tukulti-Ninib I called its name.
6. In the midst thereof a temple for the gods Ashur, and Adad, and Shamash, and Ninib, and Nusku,
7. and Nergal, and Imina-bi, and Ishtar, the great gods, my lords,
8. I completed. A direct canal for the shrines thereof

Rev.
1. *ša ṣi-i* ^{ilu}*Šam-še mi-ṣir mâti-ia aš-ku-un*
2. *ina u-mi-šu-ma e-bir-ti*[1] *ali-ia* ^{ilu}*A-šur* ^{ilu}*Bêl bêlu ma-ha-za.*
3. *e-ri-ša-ni-ma e-piš ad-ma-ni-šu*[2] *ik-ba-a*
4. *i-ta-at*[3] *ba-it ilâni*^{pl} *ma-ha-za rabâ(a) šu-bat šarru-ti-ia*
5. *ab-ni*^{alu}*Kar-*^m*Tukulti(ti)-* ^{ilu}*Ninib šum-šu ab-bi*
6. *ina kir-bi-šu bît* ^{ilu}*A-šur* ^{ilu}*Adad* ^{ilu}*Šamaš* ^{ilu}*Nin-ib* ^{ilu}*Nusku*
7. ^{ilu}*Nergal* ^{ilu}*Imina-bi u* ^{ilu}*Ištar ilâni*^{pl} *rabûti*^{pl} *bêlê*^{pl}*-ia*
8. *u-šik-lil pa-at-tu me-ša-ri a-na iš-ri-ti-šu*

[2] The signs ⟩⟩ and ⟨ are cut over an erasure.
[3] When used as a preposition, *i-ta-at*, the plur. of *ittu*, "side," has elsewhere the meaning, "beside, around."

REV.

9.

10.

11.

12.

13.

14.

15.

16.

---

[1] The plural *ḳa-ḳa-ra-te* is of interest, as *ḳaḳḳaru* is elsewhere used in the singular.

[2] The meaning of the phrase *i-ta-at* *ᵢˡᵘNabû* is not quite clear. The group AN-SA = Nabû (*cf.* Brünnow, No. 2291), but in the list of temples

REV.

9. I opened, and through the abundance of water from that canal

10. regular offerings for the great gods, my lords, for ever

11. did I establish.   In the midst of that city earth

12. in abundance beside the god Nabu [2] did I set, and for one hundred and twenty tikpi

13. on high I piled it.[3]   Above those tikpi

14. a palace corresponding to the size thereof, a mighty house, I built for my royal habitation.

15. At that time the wall of Kar-Tukulti-Ninib, the great city,

16. the fortress [4] of my dominion, I built, and from the foundation

REV.

9. *uš-pil-ki ina ḫi-ṣi-ib mê*[pl] *pa-at-ti šu-a-ti*

10. *gi-na-a ana ilâni*[pl] *rabûti*[pl] *bêlê*[pl]-*ia ana da-ri-iš*

11. *lu ar-ku-us ina ki-rib ma-ḫa-zi ša-a-tu ka-ka-ra-te*[1]

12. *ma-da-te i-ta-at* [ilu]*Nabû*[2] *aṣ-bat II šu-ši ti-ik-pi*

13. *a-na e-li-na lu-be-lit*[3] *e-li-en ti-ik-pi ša-tu-nu*

14. *ekal me-ḫi-ra bît kiš-ša-ti šu-bat šarru-ti-ia ab-ni*

15. *ina u-mi-šu-ma dûr* [alu]*Kar-*[m]*Tukulti(ti)-*[ilu]*Ninib ma-ḫa-zi rabî(i)*

16. *ri-ši-ib-tu*[4] *be-lu-ti-ia e-pu-uš iš-tu uš-še-šu*

---

which Tukulti-Ninib built, there is not one dedicated to him; had there been, the phrase might be explained as meaning "beside the temple of Nabû." It should possibly be rendered, "at the word of Nabû"; *cf. i-ta-at ba-it ilâni*[pl] in Rev., l. 4.

[3] The verb *lu-be-lit* may probably be taken as II 1, from the verb *balâtu*, "to abound," with the meaning "to pile up, to heap up."

[4] The meaning, "fortress," may probably be assigned to the substantive *rišibtu*; it is a derivative of the root *rašâbu*, "to be mighty."

Rev.

17. 𒀭 𒈗 𒄿 𒐊 𒈗 𒂍 𒈗 𒂊

18. 𒀭 𒐊 𒈗 𒐊 𒐊 𒈗 𒐊

19. 𒈗 𒐊 𒐊 𒐊 𒈗 𒈗[2] 𒐊 𒐊 𒐊[3] 𒐊 𒐊 𒈗

20. 𒐊 𒐊 𒈗 𒈗 𒈗 𒈗 𒈗

21. 𒀭 𒐊 𒈗 𒐊 𒈗 𒈗 𒐊 𒐊 𒐊 𒐊 𒐊 𒐊

22. 𒐊 𒈗 𒐊 𒈗 𒈗 𒐊 𒐊 𒈗

23. 𒐊 𒐊 𒐊 𒈗 𒐊 𒐊 𒐊 𒐊 𒐊 𒐊

24. 𒐊 𒐊 𒈗 𒐊 𒈗 𒐊 𒐊 𒐊 𒐊 𒈗

Rev.

17. unto the coping thereof I completed it, and my memorial-tablet have I set in place.

18. In the days that are to come may a future prince, when this wall

19. shall have grown old and shall have fallen in ruins, repair the damaged parts thereof,

20. and may he anoint my memorial-tablet with oil, and may he offer sacrifices,

21. and restore it unto its place, and then Ashur will hearken unto his prayers.

22. But whosoever shall destroy this wall, or shall remove my memorial-tablet

23. or my name that is inscribed thereon, or shall leave deserted or shall destroy Kar-Tukulti-Ninib,

24. the city of my dominion,

Rev.

17. *a-di taḫ-lu-[bi]-šu[1] u-šik-lil u na-ri-ia aš-ku-un*

18. *a-na arkât ûmê[pl] rubû ar-ku-u e-na-ma du-ru*

19. *šu-u u-šal-ba-ru-ma[2] e-na-ḫu[3] an-ḫu-su lu-di-iš*

20. *na-ri-ia šamni lip-šu-uš ni-ḳa-a liḳ-ḳi*

21. *a-na aš-ri-šu lu-tir [ilu]A-šur ik-ri-be-šu i-še-me*

22. *ša dûru ša-a-tu i-a-ba-tu-ma na-ri-a*

23. *u šumi šaṭ-ra u-ša-sa-ku [alu]Kar-[m]Tukulti(i)- [ilu]Ninib*

24. *ma-ḫa-az be-lu-ti-ia u-maš-ša-ru-ma*

---

[1] The signs 𒀭𒇻 𒆷 are written over an erasure. The engraver has evidently omitted the sign 𒌑 by mistake.

[2] The signs 𒁀 and 𒊒 are written over erasures.

[3] The word 𒂊 𒈾 𒄷 is written over an erasure.

Rev.

25.

26.

27.

28.

29.

30.

Rev.

25. may the lord Ashur overthrow his kingdom,
26. and may he break his weapons, and may he cause his warriors to be defeated,
27. and may he diminish his boundaries,
28. and may he ordain that his rule shall be cut off, and on his days
29. may he bring sorrow, and his years may he make evil, and his name and his seed
30. may he blot out from the land!

Rev.

25. *i-na-du-u* ^{ilu}*A-šur bêlu šarru-su lis-kip*
26. *kakkê^{pl}-šu lu-še-bir a-bi-ik-ti ṣâbê^{pl}-šu*
27. *liš-ku-un mi-iṣ-ri-ti-šu lu-ṣi-ḫi-ir*
28. *u ḳi-it palê^{pl} li-ši-ma-šu ûmê^{pl}-šu*
29. *lu-ud-ḫi šanâti^{pl}-šu lu-li-mi-in šum-šu u zêr-šu*
30. *i-na mâti lu-ḫal-liḳ*

(96)

II.

SUPPLEMENTARY TEXTS.

1. PASSAGE FROM A TABLET OF THE "BABYLONIAN CHRONICLE" RECORDING THE DEFEAT OF BIBEIASHU, KING OF BABYLON, BY TUKULTI-NINIB I, AND THE LATTER'S RULE IN BABYLONIA.

[82–7-4, 38, Col. IV, ll. 1–13.]

COL. IV.

1. [· · · · · · · · · 𒀭] 𒌁 𒄿𒆤 𒀭𒆤 𒁹 𒌅 𒃻
   [· · · · · · · · ·]²

2. [· · · · · · · · · · 𒂠] 𒀀𒋾 𒄿𒋾 𒀲𒆠𒈾 [· · · · · · · · ·]

3. [· · · · · · · · 𒁹 𒂍] 𒆤𒄿𒋾 𒌁𒀀𒄿 𒁹𒄿 𒌌 𒈬𒀸 𒆪 𒀀𒈠 𒀀𒊏 𒍝 𒅆

4. [· · · · · · · · 𒂠] 𒄩 𒀭𒋛 𒀀 𒂍𒁀 𒌌 𒈬𒀸 𒆪 𒄿𒆤 𒀀𒋾 𒅆 𒌌 𒈬𒀸 𒆪 𒄿 𒀀𒋾 𒂍

5. [𒄿𒆤] 𒀀𒋾 𒌋 𒀀𒈾𒋼 𒀭𒋛 𒀀𒋼𒉿 𒁾 𒆠 𒌌 𒈬𒀸 𒆪 𒄿 𒊏 𒀀𒆷 𒀸 𒅖𒋾 𒃻𒋻 𒅅𒋻 𒀀𒋾 𒆗𒈾

Col. IV.
1. [. . . . .] the defeat of Bibe[iashu]²
2. [he accomplished . . . .] before the god Ninib
   he set [. . . . .]
3. [. . . . . Tukulti]-Ninib returned to Babylon
   and
4. [. . . . .] they drew nigh.   He destroyed the
   wall of Babylon, and the men of Babylon he
   slew with the sword.
5. The treasures or Esagil and of Babylon he pro-
   fanely brought forth, and the great lord Marduk

Col. IV.
1. [. . . . . *a*]-*bi-ik-ti* ᵐ*Bi-be-*[*ia-šu*]²
2. [*iš-kun* . . . . *ma*]-*ḫar* ^{ilu}*Ninib id-di*[. . . . .]
3. [. . . . . ᵐ*Tukulti*](*ti*)-^{ilu}*Ninib a-na Bâbili*ᴷᴵ *i-tu-ra-am-ma*
4. [. . . . . *i*]-*kar-ri-bu dûr Babili*ᴷᴵ *ik-kur mâr Bâbili*ᴷᴵ *ina kakki*
5. [*ik*]-*kur makkur E-sag-gil u Bâbili*ᴷᴵ *ina sil-lat uš-te-ṣi* ^{ilu}*Bêl rabû*(*u*) ^{ilu}*Marduk*

---

¹ For a facsimile copy of the text, see below, *Cuneiform Texts*. The text has been previously published by Winckler, *Altorientalischen Forschungen*, I, p. 302 f. ; *cf.* also Pinches, *Records of the Past*, New Series, Vol. V, p. 111. For a discussion of the facts recorded by the document concerning the reign of Tukulti-Ninib I, see the Introduction, pp. 4 f., 49 f., 71 ff.
² It is possible that the name of Bibeiashu was here abbreviated to Bibe, the form under which it occurs in the Babylonian Kings' List. In that case l. 1 would read [. . . . . *a*]-*bi-ik-ti* ᵐ*Bi-be* [*iš-kun*].

COL. IV.

6. [cuneiform text]

7. [cuneiform text]

8. [cuneiform text]

9. [cuneiform text] [2]

10. [cuneiform text]

11. [cuneiform text]

---

[1] Possibly the scribe has written 𒅊 in place of 𒈙, which would give the better form *u-ša-as-siḫ*.

Col. IV.

6. he removed from his dwelling-place, and he carried him away into Assyria. The administration of his governors

7. he set up in the land of Kar-Duniash. For seven years did Tukulti-Ninib rule over Kar-Duniash.

8. Afterwards the nobles of Akkad and of Kar-Duniash revolted,

9. and they set Adad-shum-uṣur upon his father's throne. Against Tukulti-Ninib, who had brought evil upon Babylon,

10. Ashur-naṣir-pal, his son, and the nobles of Assyria revolted,

11. and from his throne they cast him, and they besieged him in a house in the city of Kar-Tukulti-Ninib, and they slew him with the sword.

Col. IV.

6. [ina] šub-ti-šu id-ki-e-ma a-na ᵐᵃᵗᵘAššurᴷᴵ u-za-as-siḫ ḫar-ra-an ᵃᵐᵉˡᵘšak-nu-ti-šu

7. ina ᵐᵃᵗᵘKar-ⁱˡᵘDun-ia-aš iš-kun 7 šanâtiᵖˡ ᵐTukulti (ti)-ⁱˡᵘNinib Kar-ⁱˡᵘDun-ia-aš

8. u-ma-'i-ir arki ᵃᵐᵉˡᵘrabûtiᵖˡ ša ᵐᵃᵗᵘAkkadîᴷᴵ ša ᵐᵃᵗᵘKaɪ-ⁱˡᵘDun-ia-aš ibbalkitûᵖˡ-ma

9. ᵐ ⁱˡᵘAdad-šum-uṣur ina kussî abi-šu u-še-ši-bu ᵐTukulti(ti)-ⁱˡᵘNinib ša ana Bâbiliᴷᴵ ana² limuttu(tu)

10. lu u-bil-lu ᵐ ⁱˡᵘAššur-na-ṣir-apli mâru-šu u ᵃᵐᵉˡᵘrabûtiᵖˡ ša ᵐᵃᵗᵘAššurᴷᴵ ibbalkitûᵖˡ-šu-ma

11. [ina] kussî-šu id-ku-šu-ma ina ᵃˡᵘKar-Tukulti(ti)-ⁱˡᵘNinib ina bîti i-si-ru-šu-ma ina kakki idûkûᵖˡ-šu

---

² It is possible that the scribe has repeated the preposition ⫶, ana, by mistake, and that the text should read either ša ana Bâbiliᴷᴵ limuttu(tu) lu u-bil-lu, or ša Bâbiluᴷᴵ ana limuttu(tu) lu u-bil-lu.

h 2

Col. IV.

12. [. .]𒀫 𒀭 𒁹⟨⟨⟨ 𒐖 𒀸 𒐕 𒂍 𒀝 𒁲 𒀀 ¹ — 𒈾 𒈬 ⟨𒂍 𒐖 𒐕 — 𒋾 𒁕 𒐕 𒂍 𒀝 𒁲 𒀀 𒀀𒁲 𒐖 𒁕

13. [𒋾] 𒀀𒁲𒅗 ⟨𒂍 𒊭𒀀 𒐡 𒈨

---

2. Passage from the "Synchronous History" referring to Bibeashu, king of Babylon, and its context.

[S. 2106, Obv., restored from K. 4401*a* + R. 854, and K. 4401*b*, Obv., Col. II, ll. 1–8.]²

S. 2106.

1. [𒐕 𒈾 𒀀 𒊮 ⟨⟨ 𒋾 𒈬 𒐕 𒀀𒁲 𒀭𒊭 𒂍⟨⟨⟨⟨ 𒉌𒌋 ⟨⟨ 𒋾 𒀭𒇷 𒅔 𒋻 𒐡

2. [𒊭𒐕 𒀀𒀝 𒐖 𒐖𒀝 𒁹 — 𒀀𒁲𒐡 𒀭𒇷𒀀 ⟨𒍣 𒐕 𒐖𒊮𒈣𒊑𒈨 𒂍𒐕 𒈨 𒀸𒁹

3. [𒐕 𒈾 𒀀 𒊮 𒀭𒊭 𒐖 𒍝] 𒀀𒁲 𒀭𒐕 𒌋 𒐕 𒀀𒐕 𒀀𒁲𒐡 𒀭𒊭 𒂍⟨⟨⟨⟨ 𒉌𒌋 𒐡𒐕 𒀀𒁲𒀀𒀝

---

¹ Bêl, *i.e.*, the title of Marduk, has been taken by previous translators of the tablet as part of the preceding proper name, which was rendered as Tukulti-Ashur-Bêl. But it is the subject of the verbs *a-sib* and *it-tal-kam* (l. 13), and the meaning of the passage is that the statue of Marduk, which

Col. IV.

12. For [. . . .]-six years, until the time of Tukulti-
Ashur, Bêl[1] dwelt in Assyria; in the time of
Tukulti-Ashur did Bêl

13. go unto Babylon.

Col. IV.

12. [. . . . .]6 *šanâti^{pl} a-di ^{m}Tukulti-^{ilu}Aššur ^{ilu}Bêl[1] ina
^{mâtu}Aššur^{ki} a-šib ana tar-ṣi ^{m}Tukulti(ti)-^{ilu}Aššur
^{ilu}Bêl a-na*

13. *[Bâb]ili^{ki} it-tal-kam*

S. 2106.

1. [Adad-nirari, king of Assyria], and Nazi-marattash,
king of Karduniash,

2. fought [with one another at] Kar-Ishtar of Akarsallu.

3. [Adad-nirari] defeated Nazi-marattash,

S. 2106.

1. [^{m} ^{ilu}*Adad-nirari šar* ^{mâtu}*Aššur* ^{m}]*Na-zi-marat-taš
šar* ^{mâtu}*Kar-du-ni-aš*

2. [*it-ti a-ḫa-meš ina* ^{alu}]*Kar-^{ilu}Ištar-^{m}A-kar-sa-al-lu
i-duk*

3. [^{m} ^{ilu}*Adad-nirari a-bi*]*-ik-tu ša ^{m}Na-zi-marat-taš
iš-kun*

Tukulti-Ninib had carried to Assyria (*cf.* l. 5 f.), remained there until the
time of Tukulti-Ashur, when it was restored to Babylon; see above,
p. 72, note 1.

[2] For a facsimile copy of the text, see below, *Cuneiform Texts*. The
text has been previously published by Winckler, *Untersuchungen zur
altorientalischen Geschichte*, pp. 148, 152. For a discussion of the
passage bearing on the defeat of Bibeashu, see the Introduction, p. 8.

S. 2106.

4. 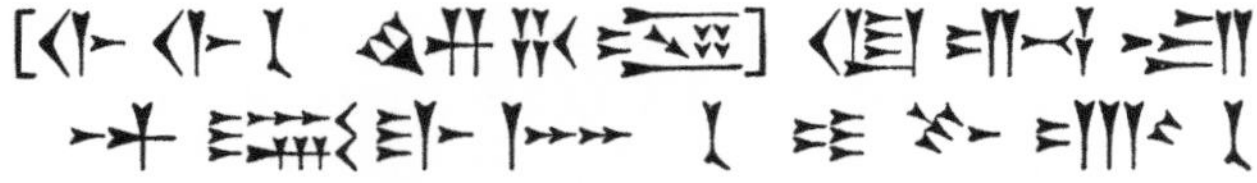

5. 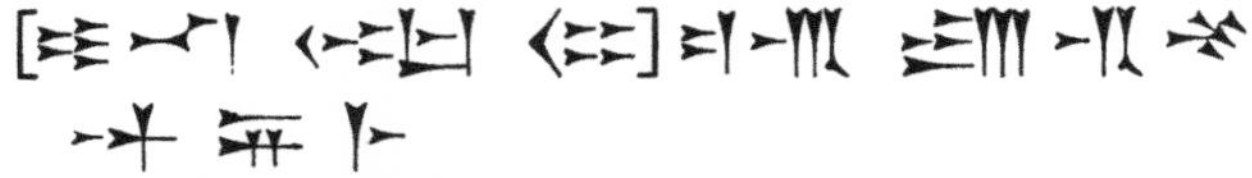

6. 

7. 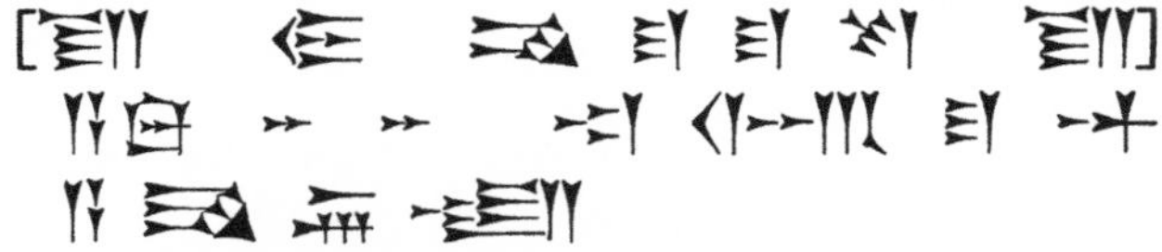

8. 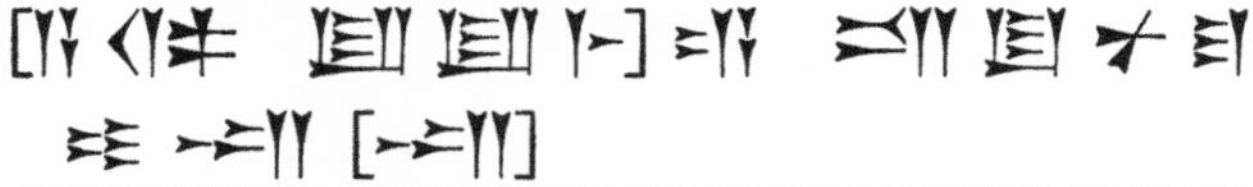

9. 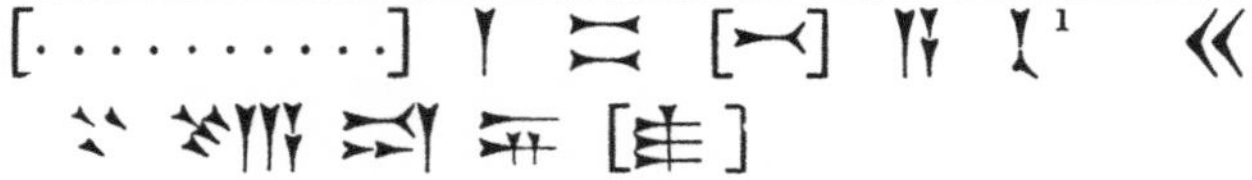

10. 

11. [. . . . .]

---

[1] On the tablet there is only room for the sign  between  and 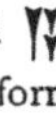, and we cannot restore the name as . Thus the form of the name in this passage of the "Synchronous History" agrees with that given in Tukulti-Ninib's annals, where it is written 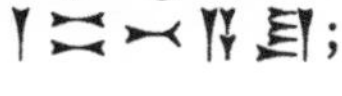; see above, p. 86.

S. 2106.

4. [and he smote him], and his camp and his priests
   he captured from him.
5. [Concerning] the boundary (they agreed) as follows :
6. [Their boundary] from the land of Pilaski,
7. [which is on the further side of] the Tigris, (from)
   the city of Arman-Akarsali
8. as far as Lulumê they established, and (thus) they
   divided it.

9. [. . . . .] Bi[be]ashu,[1] king of Karduni[ash],[2]
10. [. . . . .] in the midst of the fight
11. [. . . .]

S. 2106.

4. [*pânâtu-šu im-ḫa-aṣ*] *karas-su* *ᶦˡᵘurigallêᵖˡ-šu i-bu-
   ga-šu*
5. [*i-na eli mi*]*-iṣ-ri ta-ḫu-mu an-ni-me*
6. [*mi-ṣir-ri-šu-nu*] *iš-tu tar-ṣi* *ᵐᵃᵗᵘPi-la-as-ki*
7. [*ša šêp am-ma-ma-te ša*] *ⁿᵃʳᵘIdiglat* *ᵃˡᵘAr-ma-an-
   A-kar-sa-li*
8. [*a-di Lu-lu-me*]*-e iš-ku-nu-ma i-zu-[zu]*

9. [. . . . .] *ᵐBi-[be]-a-šu*[1] *šar* *ᵐᵃᵗᵘKar-du-ni-[aš]*[2]
10. [. . . .] *i-na ki-rib tam-ḫa-[ri]*
11. [. . . .]

[2] It is clear that this section of the "Synchronous History" corresponds
to that in the Babylonian Chronicle, 82–7–4, 38, Col. IV, ll. 1–13 (see
above, pp. 96 ff.). We may infer that it described the defeat of Bibeashu
by Tukulti-Ninib and the latter's rule in Babylon ; but it probably omitted
the details given by the Chronicle of the deportation of the statue of Bêl
to Assyria and the length of time it remained there.

[. . . . .]¹

K. 4401*b.*

1. 𒀭 𒁹 𒀭 𒀭 𒀭 𒀭 [. . . . . . .]

2. 𒀭 𒀭 𒀭 𒀭 𒀭 𒀭 [. . . . .]

3. 𒁹 𒀭 𒀭 𒀭 𒀭 𒀭 𒀭 𒀭 𒀭
𒁹 𒀭 [. . . . .]

4. 𒀭 𒀭 𒀭 𒁹 𒀭 𒀭 𒀭 𒀭 𒀭
𒁹 𒀭 𒀭 [. . . . .]

5. 𒀭   𒀭 𒀭 𒀭 𒀭 𒀭
𒁹 𒀭 𒀭 𒀭 𒀭 [. . . . .]

6. 𒀭 𒀭 𒀭 𒀭 𒀭 𒀭 𒀭 𒀭
𒀭 [. . . . .]

7. 𒀭 𒀭 𒀭 𒀭 𒀭 𒀭 𒀭
𒀭 𒀭 𒀭 𒀭 𒀭 -[. . . . .]

8. 𒀭 𒀭 𒀭 𒁹 𒀭 𒀭 𒀭 𒀭 𒀭
[. . . . .]

---

¹ Not many lines are missing in the gap between S. 2106 and K. 4401*b.*
Ll. 9–11 of S. 2106 would correspond to ll. 1–3 of Col. II of the main
tablet of the "Synchronous History" (K. 4401*a* + R. 854). The last
thirty-seven lines of this column are preserved by the main tablet, the top
half of which is missing. The thirteen lines of K. 4401*b* go in this gap,
about ten or fifteen lines before what is preserved by Col. II. Thus there
is only room for a gap of three or four lines between S. 2106 and K. 4401*b.*
It is probable that the first two lines of K. 4401*b* form the end of the
section following that which referred to Tukulti-Ninib and Bibeashu.

[..]¹

K. 4401b.

1. his slaves he made [........................]
2. as far as the city of Kullar[..................]

---

3. Bêl-kudur-uṣur, king of Assyria, and [Adad-shum-
   uṣur, king of Karduniash],
4. fought. Bêl-kudur-uṣur did Ada[d-shum-uṣur ...
   ......]
5. slay in the battle, and Ninib-apil-E[kur ....]
6. returned unto his own land. His [numerous] forces
   [he (*i.e.*, Adad-shum-uṣur) summoned],
7. and he marched against the city of Ashur to
   conquer it [..........],
8. and he fought therein, and turned, and [went back
   unto his own land].

[..]¹

K. 4401b.

1. *ᵃᵐᵉˡᵘardâniᵖˡ-šu e-pu-uš* [....................]
2. *a-di ᵃˡᵘKul-la-ar-* [..........................]

---

3. *ᵐ ⁱˡᵘBêl-ku-dur-uṣur šar ᵐᵃᵗᵘAššur ᵐ ⁱˡᵘ[Adad-šum-
   uṣur šar ᵐᵃᵗᵘKar-du-ni-aš]*
4. *i-du-ku ᵐ ⁱˡᵘBêl-ku-dur-uṣur ᵐ ⁱˡᵘAda[d-šum-uṣur ...
   ......]*
5. *ina kabal-ti [i-]du-ku-ma ᵐ ⁱˡᵘNinib-apil-E-[kur ....
   ......]*
6. *a-na mâti-šu itûr ummâni-ᵖˡ-šu ma-['a-du-ti id-ki-ma]*
7. *a-na ᵃˡᵘAššur a-na ka-ša-di il-l[i-ka ....]*
8. *ina ki-rib-šu im-ḫaṣ is-ḫur-m[a a-na mâti-šu itûr]*

3. SEAL-INSCRIPTION OF TUKULTI-NINIB I FROM A CLAY
TABLET OF THE TIME OF SENNACHERIB.

[K. 2673].[1]

OBV.

1. [cuneiform signs]

2. [cuneiform signs] [2]

3. [cuneiform signs] [3]

4. [cuneiform signs]

5. [cuneiform signs]

---

[1] For a facsimile copy of the text, see below, *Cuneiform Texts.* The text has been previously published by Rawlinson, *Cun. Inscr. West. Asia,* Vol. III, pl. 4, No. 2, and by Budge and King, *Annals of the Kings of Assyria,* pp. 14 ff.

[2] The original seal must have read [sign] not [sign], and the scribe has made a mistake in copying the sign. The form *mu-ni-kir* for the II, 1 Part. of *nakâru* is of frequent occurrence on the bowl-inscriptions of early Assyrian kings; see below, *Appendix.* In this word, and in the line upon the edge of the tablet (repeated in l. 4 of the reverse), the scribe has copied the archaic characters of the original text and has not turned them

OBV.

1. "Tukulti-Ninib, king of hosts, son of Shalmaneser, king of Assyria.
2. "Booty from the land of Kardu[nishi].   Whosoever altereth [2] my inscription or my name,
3. "may Ashur and Adad destroy his name and his land." [3]
4. This seal the enemy carried away from Assyria to Akkad.
5. But I, Sennacherib, king of Assyria,

OBV.

1. [^{ilu}]*Tukulti-Ninib šar kiššati apil* ^{ilu}*Šulmânu(nu)-ašaridu šar* ^{mâtu}*Aššur*
2. *kišitti(ti)* ^{mâtu}*Kar-du mu-[ni]-²kir siṭri-ia šumi-ia*
3. *Aššur* ^{ilu}*Adad šum-šu mât-su lu-ḫal-li-ḳu* [3]
4. ^{abnu}*kunukku an-nu-u ištu* ^{mâtu}*Aššur ana* ^{mâtu}*Akkadû*^{ki} *gar-ri ik-ta-din*
5. *ana-ku* ^{m} ^{ilu}*Sin-aḫê* ^{pl}*-erba šar* ^{mâtu}*Aššur*

---

into modern Assyrian characters.   The reason seems to be that the parts of the inscription he did not understand he did not attempt to transcribe but merely reproduced what he thought he saw upon the seal.

[3] Ll. 1–3 of the obverse and ll. 1–3 of the reverse contain copies of the seal-inscription of Tukulti-Ninib I.   The line upon the edge and Rev. l. 4 contain copies of the inscription of the original owner of the seal, *i.e.*, Shagarakti-Shuriash (see the *Introduction*, pp. 66 ff.)   This repetition may be explained as follows : Sennacherib having conquered Babylon, recovered Tukulti-Ninib's seal and he ordered its history to be recorded on the seal under Tukulti-Ninib's inscription, and the tablet K. 2673 gives the rough draft of the inscription which Sennacherib desired to be engraved.   On the reverse of the tablet is a copy of the original inscriptions upon the seal ; on the obverse and edge are the original inscriptions together with Sennacherib's proposed addition to them.

Obv.

6. [cuneiform signs]

7. [cuneiform signs]

Edge. [cuneiform signs] [1]

Rev.

1. [cuneiform signs]

2. [cuneiform signs] [2]

3. [cuneiform signs]

4. [cuneiform signs] [3]

5. [cuneiform signs]

My interpretation of this line and of l. 4 of the Reverse is that they
contain the inscription of the original owner of the seal, who, if my
reading of the signs is correct, was the Kassite king of Babylon,

Obv.

6. after six hundred years, conquered Babylon,
7. and from the spoil of Babylon I brought it forth.

Edge. " Property of Shagarakti-Shuriash, king of hosts." ¹

Rev.

1. " Tukulti-Ninib, king of hosts, son of Shalman[eser], king of Assyria.
2. "[Booty] from the land of Kardunishi. Whosoever altereth² my inscription or my name,
3. " may Ashur and Adad destroy his name and his land."
4. " Property of Shagarakti-Shuriash, king of hosts."³
5. This is that which is written upon the seal of lapis-lazuli.

Obv.

6. *ina* 600 *šanâti ᵖˡ Bâb-ilu akšud(ud)-ma*
7. *ištu makkur Bâb-ili us-si-ṣi-aš-šu*

Edge. *makkur Ša-ga-ra-ak-ti-Šur-ia-aš šar kiššati*¹

Rev.

1. *ⁱˡᵘTukulti-Ninib šar kiššati apil ⁱˡᵘŠulmânu(nu)- [ašaridu] šar ᵐâᵗᵘAššur*
2. *[kišitti](ti) ᵐâᵗᵘKar-du-ni-ši mu-[ni]²-kir šitri-ia šumi-ia*
3. *Aššur ⁱˡᵘAdad šum-šu mât-su lu-ḫal-li-ku*
4. *makkur Ša-ga-ra-ak-ti-Šur-ia-aš šar kiššati* ⁴
5. *ša ina eli ᵃᵇⁿᵘkunukki ša uknû*

Shagarakti-Shuriash. For a full discussion of the two lines, see the *Introduction*, pp. 65 ff.
² See above p. 106, note 2.   ³ See above, note 1.

4. Accounts of the capture of Babylon by Sennacherib in 702 B.C. and 689 B.C., on one of which occasions he recovered the seal of Tukulti-Ninib I.[1]

A.—The Capture of Babylon in 702 B.C.

[55-10-3, 1, Col. I, ll. 19-36.][2]

Col. I.

19. 𒁹 𒁹 𒁹 𒁹 𒁹 𒁹 𒁹 𒁹 𒁹 𒁹 𒁹 𒁹

20. 𒁹 𒁹 𒁹 𒁹 𒁹 𒁹 𒁹 𒁹 𒁹 𒁹 𒁹 𒁹 𒁹 𒁹 𒁹

21. 𒁹 𒁹 𒁹 𒁹 𒁹 𒁹 𒁹 𒁹 𒁹 𒁹 𒁹 𒁹

22. 𒁹 𒁹 𒁹 𒁹 𒁹 𒁹 𒁹 𒁹 𒁹 𒁹 𒁹 𒁹 𒁹

23. 𒁹 𒁹 𒁹 𒁹 𒁹 𒁹 𒁹 𒁹 𒁹 𒁹

24. 𒁹 𒁹 𒁹 𒁹 𒁹 𒁹 𒁹 𒁹 𒁹 𒁹 𒁹

25. 𒁹 𒁹 𒁹 𒁹 𒁹 𒁹 𒁹 𒁹 𒁹 𒁹 𒁹 𒁹 𒁹

[1] On the tablet K. 2673, Sennacherib states that he found Tukulti-Ninib's seal among the spoil of Babylon, when he captured that city, six hundred years after the seal had been carried thither from Assyria (see

Col. I.

19. In my first campaign I accomplished the overthrow of Merodach-baladan,

20. king of Kar-Duniash, together with the forces of Elam, his allies,

21. in the neighbourhood of the city of Kish.

22. In the midst of that battle he left his camp,

23. and fled alone, and saved his life.

24. The chariots, and horses, and wagons, and mules,

25. which he had deserted at the attack of my forces in battle array, my hands seized.

Col. I.

19. *i-na maḫ-ri-e gir-ri-ia ša ^{m ilu}Marduk-apil-iddina(na)*

20. *šar ^{mâtu}Kar-^{ilu}Dun-ia-aš a-di ummâni Elamti^{ki} ri-ṣi-šu*

21. *i-na ta-mir-ti Kiš^{ki} aš-ta-kan abikta-šu*

22. *i-na kabal tam-ḫa-ri šu-a-tu e-zib karas-su*

23. *e-diš ip-par-šid-ma na-piš-tuš e-ṭi-ir*

24. *narkabâti^{pl} sisê^{pl} ^{isu}su-um-bi parê^{pl}*

25. *ša i-na kit-ru-ub ta-ḫa-zi u-maš-še-ru ik-šu-da kâtâ^{II}-a-a*

above pp. 106 ff.). In the two passages from Sennacherib's prism in the British Museum and from his inscriptions in the gorge of the Gomel near Bavian, which are here printed and translated, accounts are given of the two occasions on which Sennacherib captured Babylon. For a discussion of these passages and their bearing upon the date of Tukulti-Ninib I, see the *Introduction*, p. 64 f.

² *Cf.* Rawlinson, *Cuneiform Inscriptions of Western Asia*, Vol. I, pl. 37.

COL. I.

26.

27.

28.

29.

30.

31.

32.

33.

34.

---

[1] Var. , 75, , 89.

COL. I.

26. Into his palace which is in the midst of Babylon I entered joyfully,
27. and I opened his treasure-house.   Gold, and silver,
28. and precious vessels of gold and silver of every kind,
29. and property and possessions without number, a heavy spoil, and his palace-women,
30. and (his) high officers and attendants, and (his) male and female musicians,
31. and all the servants, as many as there were,
32. who ministered in his palace, I brought forth,
33. and I counted them as spoil.   Through the might of Ashur, my lord,
34. seventy-six [1] of his strongly fortified cities in the land of Kaldi [2]

COL. I.

26. *a-na ekalli-šu ša ki-rib Bâbili*^{KI} *ḫa-diš e-ru-um-ma*
27. *ap-te-e-ma bît ni-ṣir-ti-šu ḫurâṣu kaspu*
28. *u-nu-tu ḫurâsi kaspi a-kar-tu mimma šum-šu*
29. *bušû makkuru la ni-ba ka-bit-tu biltu ṣ libbi-ekalli*^{pl}*-šu*
30. ^{amêlu}GAL-TE^{pl} ^{amêlu}*man-za-az-pa-ni* ^{amêlu}*zammerê*^{pl} *'zammerêti*^{pl}
31. *si-ḫir-ti um-ma-a-ni ma-la ba-šu-u*
32. *mut-tab-bi-lu-ut ekallu-uš u-še-ṣa-am-ma*
33. *šal-la-ti-iš am-nu i-na e-muk* ^{ilu}*Aššur bêli-ia*
34. *76* [1] *alâni*^{pl}*-šu dan-nu-ti bît dûrâni*^{pl}*(ni) ša* ^{mâtu}*Kal-di* [2]

---

[2] The lines here quoted, which give the numbers of the cities captured by Sennacherib in Babylonia, are followed by a list of the principal ones among them.   In ll. 40–62, which complete the account of the campaign, Sennacherib records the conquests made on the march back to Assyria, and he gives a list of the spoil and tribute he took back with him.

i

COL. I.

35. 𒀭𒂗𒇹 𒀸 𒁹 𒐏 [1] ⸱⸱⸱ 𒌋

      𒆤 𒁹⸱⸱⸱ 𒂗𒇹 ⸱⸱𒂗𒇹 𒁹 ⸱𒅗 𒀸 𒀖

36. 𒂊𒆤 𒁹 ⸱𒁀 𒊹𒈨𒈨 𒀀𒅀   𒇀 𒂗𒇹 ⸱𒂗

      𒀪 ⸱𒂗 ⸱𒂗𒇹 𒂍𒅊

B.—THE CAPTURE OF BABYLON IN 689 B.C.

[From the inscriptions of Sennacherib near Bavian in Assyria.] [2]

BAV. INSCR.

43. 𒇷 𒅆𒁹 𒐊 𒇷 [3] 𒅖 𒂗𒇹 𒐊 𒅆𒁹

      𒂗𒆠 ⸱𒀸 𒂗𒇹 𒀭   𒀸 [4] 𒐊 𒅆𒁹

      ⸱𒁍 𒀸 𒀸 𒈨𒁹 𒐊 𒁀 𒁹𒀭 𒂗

      𒀀 𒈨𒅀 𒀖 𒁹

44. 𒂊𒆤 𒈨 𒂗 𒀭 𒂗 ⸱𒅗 𒈨𒁹

      𒁹 𒀀 𒂗𒇹 𒐊 𒐏𒌍 𒂗 𒀭 𒁉

      𒀀𒈨 𒂗 ⸱𒐊𒅗 𒁾𒈨 ⸱𒅗 𒂗𒆤 𒂗𒇹 [5]

      ⸱𒂗𒇹 𒌋 𒇷 ⸱𒅗 𒂊𒆤 𒁹 𒂗 𒇷 ⸱𒅀

---

[1] Var. 𒐊 𒁹 𒐏, 820.

[2] The text is taken from my own edition of the Bavian Inscriptions, made in the spring of the year 1894; the text is based on the inscribed tablet which is highest up the gorge (referred to as A), and is restored from the other two duplicate tablets. The central inscribed tablet is referred to as B, and that nearest to the mouth of the gorge as C. The

Col. I.

35. and four hundred and twenty[1] small cities in the neighbourhood thereof

36. I besieged, I captured, and I carried off their spoil.

Col. I.

35. *u 420*[1] *alâni^(pl)(ni) ṣiḫrûti^(pl) ša li-me-ti-šu-nu*

36. *al-me ak-šud(ud) aš-lu-la šal-la-su-un*

Bav. Inscr.

43. In my second[3] campaign unto Babylon, to conquer which I had determined, swiftly

44. I marched, and I broke loose like the onset of a storm, and like a hurricane I overwhelmed it. I invested the city with a blockading force, and with

Bav. Inscr.

43. *i-na šanî(i)*[3] *girri-ia a-na Bâbili_{KI} ša*[4] *a-na ka-ša-di u-ṣa-am-me-ru-šu ḫi-it-mu-ṭiš*

44. *al-lik-ma ki-ma ti-ib me-ḫi-e a-zik-ma ki-ma im-ba-ri as-ḫu-up-šu*[5] *ala ni-i-ti al-me-ma i-na*

---

inscriptions C, B, and A are cut on each side of figures of Sennacherib and upon the king's robe in panels IV, VIII, and XI; I have numbered the panels in the order in which they occur in the gorge as one ascends the stream of the Gomel. It may be noted that many of the difficult passages which occur in the text as published by Rawlinson in *Cun. Insc. West. Asia*, Vol. III, pl. 14, are due to misreadings of the squeezes taken by Layard. I made copies as well as squeezes of all three inscriptions on the rock and have been able to clear up many of the difficulties; *cf.*, *e.g.*, ll. 45, 47 (p. 116 f.), 52 and 53 (p. 120 f.) My edition of the inscriptions has not yet been published.

[3] *I.e.*, Sennacherib's second campaign against Babylon.

[4] B 𒂊𒐖.   [5] 𒌋.

BAV. INSCR.

45.

46.

47.

48.

---

[1] A, B, and C all read 𒐠 ⟨𒑠, not 𒐠 𒑠 as R.

BAV. INSCR.
45. mines[1] and siege-engines my hands [captured
    it . . . . .] the spoil of [. . . . .] his mighty ones
    [. . . . .] I left neither small nor great, and with
    their corpses I filled the open places of the city.
46. Shuzubu, king of Babylon, together with his family
    and his [. . . . .] alive I carried away into my land.
47. The property of that city, silver,[3] and gold, and
    precious stones, and goods, and possessions I
    handed over unto my people, and I made them
    their own possessions.
48. The gods that dwelt therein the hands of my people
    captured, and they broke them in pieces, and they
    took their goods and possessions.   Adad and
    Shala, the gods

BAV. INSCR.
45. *pil-ši* [1] *u na-bal-ka-ti kâtâ^{II}-[a-a . . . .]*
    ḫu-bu-ut [. . . . .] *dannûti^{pl}-šu ṣiḫra u rabâ(a)*
    la e-zib-ma ^{amêlu}*pagrê^{pl}-šu-nu ri-bit ali*
46. *u-mal-li* ^{m}*Šu-zu-bu šar Bâbili^{KI} ga-du kim-ti-šu*
    [. . . . .]^{pl}*-šu bal-ṭu-su-un a-na ki-rib mâti-ia*
    u-bil-la [2]
47. *makkur ali šu-a-tu kaspu* [3] *ḫurâṣu abnê^{pl} mi-sik-ti*
    bušû makkuru a-na kâtâ^{II} [niše^{pl}]*-i[a] am-ni-i-ma*
    a-na i-di ra-ma-ni-šu-nu u-tir-ru
48. *ilâni^{pl} a-šib lib-bi-šu kâtâ^{II} niše^{pl}-ia ik-šu-su-nu-ti-*
    ma u-šab-bi-ru-ma [bušû]*-šu-nu makkuru-šu-nu il-*
    ku-ni [4] ^{ilu}*Adad* ^{ilu}*Ša-la ilâni^{pl}*

_____

² B 𒂊𒁹, *u-bil-šu.*
³ This word is preserved by B and is ⟨𒌍 𒀀𒁹⟩, not 𒌋𒌋 𒀊 as R.
⁴ B 𒂍𒐉𒂊, i.e., *il-ku-u.*

BAV. INSCR.

49.

50.

51.

BAV. INSCR.

49. of the city of Ekallâti, whom Marduk-nadin-akhê, king of Akkad, at the time of Tiglath-pileser, king of Assyria, had taken and had brought unto Babylon,

50. after four hundred and eighteen years I brought forth from Babylon, and I restored them unto their place in the city of E[kallâti]. The city and the houses (thereof)

51. from the foundation unto the roof thereof I destroyed, I laid waste, I burned with fire. The inner and the outer wall, and the temples of the gods, and the temple-towers of brick and earth, all that there were,

BAV. INSCR.

49. *ša* ^{alu}*Ekallâti*^{pl} *ša* ^{m ilu}*Marduk-nadin*¹*-aḫê*^{pl 2} *šar* ^{mâtu}*Akkadî*^{KI} *a-na tar-ṣi* ^m*Tukulti(ti)-apil-E-šar-ra* [*ša*]*r*³ ^{mâtu}*Aššur*^{KI} *il-ḳu-ma a-na Bâbili*^{KI} *u-bil-lu*

50. *i-na* 418 *šanâti*^{pl} *ul-tu Bâbili*^{KI} *u-še-ṣa-am-ma a-na* ^{alu}*E[kallâti*^{pl}] *a-na aš-ri-šu-nu u-tir-šu-nu-ti ala u bitâti*^{pl}

51. *ul-tu ušši-šu a-di taḫ-lu-bi-šu ab-bul ak-kur i-na* ^{ilu}*Gibil ak-mu dûru u šal-ḫu-u bîtâti*^{pl} *ilâni*^{pl} *zig-gur-rat libitti u epiri ma-la ba-šu-u*

---

¹ So B; C 𒂊.
² So A and C; B 𒐜.
³ The end of the sign is preserved by A.

Bav. Inscr.

52. 〔cuneiform〕

53. 〔cuneiform〕

54. 〔cuneiform〕

---

[1] This passage is preserved by A and B; the signs between *i-na* and *ali* are 〔cuneiform〕, not 〔cuneiform〕, as R.

[2] The traces on B are probably those of 〔cuneiform〕, not 〔cuneiform〕.

[3] C omits 〔cuneiform〕.

BAV. INSCR.

52. I tore up, and I cast them into the Arakhtu-canal. In the midst[1] of that city I cut channels,[2] and the earth thereof I overwhelmed with water, and the structure

53. of its foundation I destroyed, and I spread abroad its brickwork[5] more than after an inundation. That in future days the site of that city and the temples of the gods

54. no man may find, I destroyed it with water and blotted it out so that it became like unto a swamp.

BAV. INSCR.

52. *as-suḫ-ma a-na* ᵃⁿ*A-ra-aḫ-ti ad-di i-na ki-rib*[1] *ali šu-a-tu ḫ[i-r]a*[2]*-a-ti aḫ-ri-e-ma ir-ṣi-is-su-nu*[3] *ina*[4] *mê*ᵖˡ *as-pu-un ši-kin*

53. *uš-še-šu u-ḫal-lik-ma eli ša a-bu-bu na-al-ban-ta-šu*[5] *u-ša-tir*[6] *aš-šu aḫ-rat u-me kak-kar ali šu-a-tu u bîtâti*ᵖˡ *ilâni*ᵖˡ

54. *la muš-ši i-na ma-a-mi uš-ḫar-mit-su-ma ag-da-mar u-šal-liš*

---

⁴ C 𒂊 𒊏, *i-na.*

⁵ This reading is quite certain; the signs 𒂊𒅗 𒀜 are clear on A and B.

⁶ C 𒋗𒂊𒐊.

APPENDIX.

THE BOWL-INSCRIPTIONS OF SHALMANESER I, KING OF ASSYRIA, ABOUT 1300 B.C.

The late Mr. George Smith, in *Assyrian Discoveries*, p. 248 f., published a translation of the contents of a bowl-inscription[1] of Shalmaneser I. He described his rendering of the text as "a restored translation," and added that "in parts the record is so mutilated that I " have only given the general sense." He did not state from how many inscribed fragments of bowls his text was taken, and, although frequent reference has been made to his translation in the works of other writers, a certain mystery has hitherto surrounded the identity of the fragments upon which it was based.

Three fragments of bowl-inscriptions of Shalmaneser I (Nos. 56–9–9, 164, 181, and 187) are published in *Cun. Inscr. West. Asia*, Vol. III, pl. 3, Nos. 3–5, and in the Index to that work (p. 5) they are described as "probably Fragments of Shalmaneser I"; but this identification has not been universally accepted. Prof. Bezold, in Vol. IV of his *Catalogue*, pp. 1693 ff., describes No. 164 as "part of an inscription of Shalmaneser(?)," and each of the others as "part of an inscription of

---

[1] In the British Museum are a number of inscriptions of Assyrian kings, which are written in circles round the outside of clay bowls and dishes. The longer inscriptions record building operations, and it is probable that the bowls were deposited as votive offerings in the temples of the gods. The inscriptions of Shalmaneser I, which are published in this appendix, were found at Kuyunjik.

an Assyrian king, probably Shalmaneser," and in Vol. V, p. 2193, he indexes them as inscriptions of Shalmaneser II, not of Shalmaneser I.

The most recent reference to the bowl-inscriptions of Shalmaneser I which I have come across occurs in the *Encyclopædia Biblica*, Vol. III (1902), Col. 3422 f., in the article "Nineveh," by the Rev. H. C. W. Johns. Here it is stated that "the earliest native notices [*i.e.*, of "Nineveh] are on the votive bowls of Shalmaneser I "(about 1300 B.C.). These short notices (*KB* I 9; "3 *R*, pl. 5, No. 3–5) are to be read in the light of "Tiglath - pileser's reminiscences of Shalmaneser "(G. Smith, *Ass. Disc.*, 248). Shalmaneser claims to "have renewed the temple of Ištar (3 *R* 5, No. 4)." Three lines later on Mr. Johns adds : "Shalmaneser I "(3 *R* 3, No. 12) relates that his father Adad-nirari "(about 1845 B.C.), after an expedition into Babylon, "brought back the gods of Babylon, Merodach and "Nebo, and built them temples."

At first sight these passages from the article by Mr. Johns would seem to dispose of the difficulty in connection with the identity of the bowl-inscriptions of Shalmaneser I, for they appear to give references to the original publications of the text.   But it must be noted that not one of the references given is correct. *KB* I 9 (= Schrader's *Keilins. Bibl.*, Bd. I, p. 9) does not give translations of the texts, nor does it even refer to them.   The texts published in 3 *R*, pl. 5, No. 3–5 (= Rawlinson's *Cun. Inscr. West. Asia*, Vol. III) are not bowl-inscriptions of Shalmaneser I, but tablet-inscriptions of Tiglath-pileser I.[1] And finally 3 R 3, No. 12, is not an inscription of Shalmaneser I, but of Sargon II, for the beginning of Sargon's name occurs in l. 1 of the text, and the characters of the inscription are those of the period of Sargon not of Shalmaneser I ; the text, in fact, records the restoration of the temple of Marduk and Nabû by Adad-nirari (probably Adad-nirari III) and afterwards by Sargon II.[2]

I think there is no doubt that Mr. George Smith used for his translation only four fragments of bowl-inscriptions of Shalmaneser I, viz., Nos. 56–9–9, 164, 181, and 187 (published in *Cun. Inscr. West. Asia,* Vol. III, pl. 3, Nos. 3–5), and the fragment S. 2115 (not since identified as an inscription of Shalmaneser I). In order to show that the most important parts of Mr. Smith's text can be obtained from these four fragments, his translation may be quoted in full and then transliterations and translations given of the separate fragments on which I think it is based. The translation given by Mr. George Smith runs :—

" Shalmaneser the powerful king, king of nations, king " of Assyria; son of Vul-nirari, the powerful king, king " of nations, king of Assyria; son of Budil, the powerful " king, king of nations, king of Assyria also. Conqueror " of . . . Niri, Lulumi . . . and Muzri, who in the service

---

[1] Possibly "pl. 5 " is a misprint for "pl. 3," but the reference is given twice, and pl. 5, No. 4, does contain a reference to Shalmaneser I. It may be added that Mr. George Smith in *Assyr. Disc.,* p. 248, does not refer to Tiglath-pileser, nor to his "reminiscences of Shalmaneser."

[2] See above, p. 59, note 2.

" of the goddess Ishtar, his lady, has marched and has
" no rival, who in the midst of battle has fought and has
" conquered their lands.   When the temple of the goddess
" Ishtar, the lady of Nineveh, my lady, which Samsi-vul,
" the prince who went before me had built, and which
" had decayed, and Assur-ubalid, my father, had restored
" it; that temple in the course of my time had decayed,
" and from its foundation to its roof I rebuilt it.   The
" prince who comes after me, who my cylinders shall see
" and restore to their place, like (sic) I the cylinders of Assur-
" ubalid have restored to their place, may Ishtar bless him ;
" and whoever destroys my records, may Ishtar curse him,
" and his name and his seed from the country root out."

The four separate fragments of bowl-inscriptions are
published as Nos. 1—4 in the Appendix to the
Cuneiform Texts and read as follows :—

No. 1 [56–9–9, 164].[1]

TRANSLITERATION.

```
[  .   .   .   .   .   .   ]   1.  [  .   .   .   .   .   .   ]
2. [  .   .   .   .   .   .   Ad]ad-nirari [  .   .   .   .   .   ]
3. [  .   .   .   .   .   .   ]-ri-i  Lu-ul-[  .   .   .   .   .   ]
4. [  .   .   .   .   .   .   I]štar bêlti-šu it-[  .   .   .   .   ]
5. [  .   .   .   .   .   -ri ]b ta-ḫa-zi il-[  .   .   .   .   .   ]
6. [  .   .   .   .   .   .   ] bît iluIštar rubât[  .   .   .   .   ]
7. [  .   .   .   .   .   .   ]iluA-šur-u-bal[liṭ  .   .   .   ]
8. [  .   .   .   .   .   .   .   .   ] u ma-aḳ-[  .   .   .   .   ]
9. [  .   .   .   .   .   .   .   .   ] u ti-m[e-  .   .   .   .   ]
   [  .   .   .   .   .   .   .   .   .   .   .   .   .   .   ]
```

[1] For the text, see below, p. 167.   The fragment measures 2⅝ in. by
3¼ in.

TRANSLATION.

```
   [ . . . . . . . ]  1.  [ . . . . . . . ]
2. [ . . . . . .   Ad]ad-nirari [ . . . . . ]
3. [ . . . . the Shuba]rî, and the Lul[lumî . . . ]
4. [ . . . . . . I]shtar, his lady, [proceedeth . . . ]
5. [ . . . in the mid]st of the battle hat[h . . . ]
6. [ . . . ] the temple of Ishtar, the princess of [ . . ]
7. [ . . . . . . ] Ashur-ubal[liṭ . . . . . . ]
8. [ . . . . . . ] and that which was [fallen . . ]
9. [ . . . . . . . ] and [my] cyl[inders . . . ]
   [ . . . . . . . . . . . . . . . . . . ]
```

No. 2 [56–9–9, 181].[1]

TRANSLITERATION.

```
   [ . . . . . . . . . . . . . . . . . ]
1. [ . . . . . . šar]ru dan-nu šar [ . . . . . . ]
2. [ . . . . . . ^{ilu}]A-šur-ma   ka-ši-[ . . . . ]
3. [ . . . . . M]u-uṣ-ri ša i-na tu-kul-ti [ . . . ]
4. [ . . . . . š]a i-na ki-rib ta-ḫa-zi il-ta-[ . . . ]
5. [ . . . e]-nu-ma bît ^{ilu}Ištar rubât(at) ^{alu}N[i- . . ]
6. [ . . . . . . . . . . . . . . . . . . . ]
   [ . . . . . . . . . . . . . . . . . . . ]
```

TRANSLATION.

```
   [ . . . . . . . . . . . . . . . . . ]
1. [ . . . . . ] the mighty king, the king of [ . . . ]
2. [ . . . . . ] of Assyria, who hath conquer[ed . . ]
3. [ . . . . . M]uṣri, who with the help of [ . . . ]
4. [ . . . ] who in the midst of the battle hath [fought ]
```

---

[1] For the text, see below, p. 167. The fragment measures 3¾ in.
by 2 in.

5. [.] when the temple of Ishtar, the queen of N[ineveh .   ]
6. [.   .   .   .   ]
   [.   .   .   .   ]

No. 3 [56–9–9, 187].[1]

TRANSLITERATION.

[.   .   .   .   ]
1. [.   .   .   .   ]
2. [.   .   .   .   .   .   ]-gi-šu-nu [.   .   .   .   .   .   ]
3. [.   .   .   .   .   N]i-na-a bêlti-i[a .   .   .   .   .   ]
4. [.   .   .   .   .   .   -b]i ud-di-šu bîtu šu-u [.   .   .   .   ]
5. [.   .   .   .   .   ] an-ša-ti-šu ak-sir u [.   .   .   .   ]
6. [.   .   .   .   .   -d]i-iš a-na aš-ri-šu-nu-ma [.   .   .   .   ]
7. [.   .   .   .   .   š]a-šu ki-ma a-na-ku-ma ti-[.   .   .   ]
8. [.   .   .   .   .   -ti]r ᶦˡᵘIštar ik-ri-bi-[.   .   .   .   .   ]
9. [.   .   .   .   .   .   -u]m-šu u [.   .   .   .   .   ]
10. [.   .   .   .   .   .   .   ]-ḫi [.   .   .   .   .   ]

TRANSLATION.

[.   .   .   .   ]
1. [.   .   .   .   ]
2. [.   .   .   .   .   ] their [.   .   .   .   .   .   .   ]
3. [.   .   .   .   .   of N]ineveh, my lady, [.   .   .   .   .   ]
4. [.   .   .   .   ] my [father] restored, that temple [.   .   ]
5. [.   .   .   .   ] the breaches thereof I filled up and [.   ]
6. [.   .   .   .   I] restored, and unto their place [.   .   .   ]
7. [.   .   .   .   ] he, even as I the cy[linders .   .   .   .   ]
8. [.   .   .   .   ] Ishtar unto [his] prayer [.   .   .   .   .   ]
9. [.   .   .   .   .   ] his [na]me and [.   .   .   .   .   ]
10. [.   .   .   .   .   .   fami]ne [.   .   .   .   .   .   ]

---

[1] For the text, see below, p. 167. The fragment measures 3⅝ in. by 3¾ in.

No. 4 [S. 2115].[1]

TRANSLITERATION.

[. . . . .]
1. [. . . . .]
2. [. . . . .] *sa* [. . . . .]
3. [. . . . .] $^{m\ ilu}$*Šamši(ši)-^{ilu}*[. . . . . .]
4. [. . . . .] *i-na ri-i-bit* [. . . . . .]
5. [. . . . . .]*iš-tu uš-ši-šu a-d*[*i* . . . .]
6. [. . . . . . *t*]*i-me-ni-ia aš-*[. . . . . .]
7. [. . . . . .]*-ni ša* $^{m\ ilu}$*A-šur-uballiṭ* [. . .]
8. [. . . . . .]*-šu i-še-*[. . . . . . .]
9. [. . . . . . *mâ*]*ti lu-ḫal-liḳ ša-a-šu* [. . .]
10. [. . . . . *-t*]*a-di*

TRANSLATION.

[. . . . .]
1. [. . . . .]
2. [. . . . .]
3. [. . . .] Shamshi-[Adad . . . .]
4. [. . . .] in the street [. . . . . .]
5. [.] from the foundation unto [the roof] thereof [.]
6. [. . . .] my cylinders I [set in place . . . .]
7. [. . . the cylind]ers of Ashur-uballiṭ [. . . .]
8. [. . . . .] unto his [prayer] will hear[ken . .]
9. [. . from the] land may he blot out, and him [.]
10. [. . . . . may] he cast!

A comparison of the above four fragments with Mr. Smith's translation shows that he took his text from the separate lines upon the fragments, and arranged them in the following order:—No. 1, l. 2 ; No. 2, l. 1 ;

---

[1] For the text, see below, p. 169.   The fragment measures 3 in. by 3 in.

k

No. 2, l. 2 ; No. 1, l. 3 ; No. 2, l. 3 ; No. 1, l. 4 ; No. 2, l. 4, and No. 1, l. 5 ; No. 3, l. 2 ; No. 2, l. 5, and No. 1, l. 6, and No. 3, l. 3 ; No. 4, l. 3 ; No. 1, l. 7 ; No. 3, l. 4 : No. 4, l. 4 (possibly) ; No. 4, l. 5 ; No. 3, l. 7 ; No. 4, l. 7 ; No. 3, l. 8, and No. 4, l. 8 ; and No. 4, l. 9 ; No. 3, l. 9 ; and No. 4, l. 10.

Certain gaps in the text Mr. Smith legitimately restored in order to carry on the sense, though he did not indicate the restorations in any way ; moreover, he seems to have ignored some of the lines upon the fragments (*e.g.*, No. 3, l. 5 ; No. 1, l. 8 ; No. 3, l. 6 ; No. 1, l. 9 ; and No. 4, l. 6), and he has thus obtained an apparently complete inscription. As a matter of fact the second half of the inscription, which is inscribed round the larger circles on the bowls, is probably longer than he makes it, and it is possible that some of the bowls give variant descriptions of the building operations. Ignoring the possibility of variant renderings, and making use of every part of the texts upon the fragments, we may obtain the following text, the portions within brackets marking the restorations :—

TRANSLITERATION.

[*m ilu*Šulmânu(*nu*)-*ašaridu šarru rabû šarru dan-nu šar kiššati šar ᵐᵃᵗᵘ ⁱˡᵘA-šur apil ᵐ ⁱˡᵘAd*]*ad-nirari*[1] [*šarru rabû šar*]*ru dan-nu šar*[2] [*kiššati šar* ᵐᵃᵗᵘ ⁱˡᵘ*A-šur apil* ᵐ*Pu-di-ilu šarru rabû šarru dan-nu šar kiššati šar* ᵐᵃᵗᵘ ⁱˡᵘ]*A-šur-ma ka-ši*[3]*-[id* . . . . *Šu-ba*]-*ri-i Lu-ul*[4]*-[lu-mi-i* . . . .

---

[1] No. 1, l. 2.   [2] No. 2, l. 1.   [3] No. 2, l. 2.   [4] No. 1, l. 3.

M]*u-uṣ-ri ša i-na tu-kul-ti*[1][*iluI*]*štar bêlti-šu it-*[2] [*tal-la-ku-ma*
ša-nin-šu la i-šu-u šarru š]*a i-na ki-rib ta-ḫa-zi il-ta*[3]-[*na-an-*
ma . . . .]-*gi-šu-nu*[4] [. . . . . *e*]-*nu-ma bît* [ilu]*Ištar*
rubât(at) [alu]*Ni-na-a bêlti-i*[*a*[5] *ša*] [m ilu]*Šam-ši-*[ilu][*Adad*[6] . . . . .
. . . . .[7] *e-pu-šu* . . . . [m][ilu]*A-šur-u-bal*[*liṭ*[8] *a-b*]*i ud-di-*
šu bîtu šu-u[9] [. . . . .] *i-na ri-i-bit*[10] [*e-na-aḫ-ma* . . . . .
. . . . .] *an-ša-ti-šu ak-sir u ma-aḳ-*[*te*[11] . . . . *ud*]-*di-iš*
a-na aš-ri-šu-nu-ma[12] [. . . . .] *iš-tu uš-ši-šu a-di*[13] [*taḫ-*
lu-bi-šu u-šik-lil . . . . *na-ri-ia*] *u ti-me-ni-ia aš*[14]-[*ku-un*
rubû arkû an-ḫu-su lu-ud-diš . . . .] *ša-šu ki-ma a-na-*
ku-ma ti[15]-[*me*]-*ni ša* [m ilu]*A-šur-uballiṭ*[16] [*ti-me-ni-ia a-na aš-ri-*
šu-nu lu-ti]*r* [ilu]*Ištar ik-ri-bi-šu i-še-*[17] [*me mu-ni-kir ši-iṭ-ri-ia u*
šu-mi-ia [ilu]*Adad šu-u*]*m-šu u*[18] [*zêr-šu i-na mâ*]*ti lu-ḫal-liḳ ša-a-*
šu[19] [. . . . . *a-na mâti-šu ḫu-ša*]-*ḫi*[20] [*lit-t*]*a-di*[21]

TRANSLATION.

[Shalmaneser, the great king, the mighty king, the king of
hosts, the king of Assyria, the son of Ad]ad-nirari, [the great
king], the mighty king, the king of [hosts, the king of Assyria,
the son of Pudi-ilu, the great king, the mighty king, the king
of hosts, the king of] Assyria, who hath conquer[ed . . . . .

---

[1] No. 2, l. 3.   [2] No. 1, l. 4.
[3] No. 2, l. 4 and No. 1, l. 5.   [4] No. 3, l. 2.
[5] No. 2, l. 5, and No. 1, l. 6, and No. 3, l. 3.
[6] No. 4, l. 3.
[7] Smith restored here the phrase *šarru a-lik pa-ni-ia.*
[8] No. 1, l. 7.   [9] No. 3, l. 4.   [10] No. 4, l. 4.
[11] No. 3, l. 5 and No. 1, l. 8.   It is probable that some of the phrases
that follow are alternative readings.
[12] No. 3, l. 6.   [13] No. 4, l. 5.
[14] No. 1, l. 9 and No. 4, l. 6.   [15] No. 3, l. 7.
[16] No. 4, l. 7.   [17] No. 3, l. 8 and No. 4, l. 8.
[18] No. 3, l. 9.   [19] No. 4, l. 9.   [20] No. 3, l. 10.   [21] No. 4, l. 10.

the Shuba]rî, and the Lul[lumî . . . . . and M]uṣri, who with
the help of [I]shtar, his lady [proceedeth and hath not a rival,
the king] who in the midst of the battle hath [fought and
. . . . .] their [. . . . .]   When the temple of Ishtar, the
queen of Nineveh, my lady, [which] Shamshi-[Adad . . . . .
had built, ... and] Ashur-ubal[liṭ], my [father] restored,
that temple [. . . . .] in the street [had fallen into ruins, and
. . . . .] the breaches thereof I filled up and that which was
[fallen . . . . . I] restored, and unto their place [. . . . .] from
the foundation unto [the roof] thereof [I completed it . . . . .
and my memorial inscriptions] and my cylinders I set [in
place. May a future prince rebuild the ruins thereof . . . . .
and may] he [restore my cylinders unto their place], even as I
(have restored) the cylinders of Ashur-uballiṭ, and then will
Ishtar hearken unto his prayer. [But whosoever shall alter
my inscription or my name (which is thereon)], may [Adad]
blot out his [na]me and [his seed from the] land, and
him [may he . . . . , and upon his land may he] cast
[fami]ne !

In addition to this inscription of Shalmaneser I,
which is written upon fragments of four bowls, and
records the restoration of the great temple of Ishtar at
Nineveh, two[1] other of his building inscriptions are
found upon fragments of bowls in the British Museum,
and are here published for the first time.   In the
following pages the fragments are transliterated and
translated in the order in which they are arranged in
the Cuneiform Texts.

---

[1] Nos. 5 and 7; on No. 6 the name of the king is wanting, but the
genealogy in l. 5 may be that of Tukulti-Ninib I.

No. 5 [S. 2125].[1]

TRANSLITERATION.

1. [^{m} ^{ilu}Šulmânu(n]u)-ašaridu
2. [. . . .] dan-nu šar [. . . . .]
3. [. . . . ka]-šu-uš ilâni^{pl} [. . . . . . .]
4. [. . . . .]-še ḫur-ša-ni [. . . . . . .]
5. [. . . . . . . T]UM Lu-ul-lu-mi-i [. . . .]
6. [. . . . . ša-a]k-ni ^{ilu}Bêl šangûAšš[ur . .]
7. [. . . . . . .]-te ša-a-ti iš-t[u . . . . .]
8 [. . . . . b]i(?)-na e-pu-uš bâb [.]
9. [. . . . .] lib(?)-be-šu [. . .]
10. [. . . . .]
[. . . . .]

TRANSLATION.

1. [Shalman]eser,
2. [. . .] the mighty [king], the king of [. . .]
3. [. . . .] the strong one of the gods [. . . .]
4. [. . . . . .] the highlands [. . . . .]
5. [. . . . . . .] the Lullumê [. . . . .]
6. [. . . the go]vernor of Bêl, the priest of Ash[ur .]
7. [. . . .] that [. .] from [. . . . .]
8. [. . . .] I built. The Gate of [. . . .]
9. [. . . . . . .] therein(?) [. . . . . .]
10. [. . . . .]
[. . . . .]

---

[1] For the text, see below, p. 169. The fragment measures 2½ in. by 3 in.

No. 6 [56–9–9, 180].[1]

Transliteration.

1. [. . . . *ša*]*r kib-rat arba'i ka-šid*[. . . . .]
2. [. . . . (*U-*)*k*]*u-ma-ni-i u Kur-*[*ṭi-i* . . . .]
3. [. . . .]*mu-si-pi-iḫ limuttu*(*t*[*u*)²]² . . . . .]
4. [. . . .]*-ud* ³ *pa-da-ni a-di pa-*[. . . . .]
5. [. *matuAš*]*šur apil Adad-nirari šar* *matuAššur-ma*[.]
6. [. . . . . *u-n*]*i-kir eš-ri-ti-šu u-še-*[. . . .]
7. [. . . . *u*]*-šik-lil u na-ri-ia aš-ku-un* [. . . .]
8. [. . *mu-n*]*i-kir šiṭ-ri-ia u šumi-ia* *iluilu*[*Adad* . . .]
9. [. . *ina m*]*âti lu-ḫal-lik*

Translation.

1. [. ki]ng of the four quarters (of the world), who hath
   conquered [. .]
2. [. . . the (U)k]umanî and the Kur[tî . . . .]
3. [. . . .] who hath made an end of evil [. . .]
4. [. . . . . .] paths as far as [. . . . .]
5. [. of As]syria, the son of Adad-nirari, king of Assyria [.]
6. [. . . I] altered the shrines thereof, I [. . . .]
7. [. I] completed, and my memorial tablets I set in
   place [. .]
8. [. But whosoever] shall alter my inscription or my name
   (which is thereon), may [Adad . .]
9. [. . and from the] land may he blot him out!

---

[1] For the text, see below, p. 171. The fragment measures 3¾ in. by
4⅛ in. ; it is possibly part of a bowl of Tukulti-Ninib I.

[2] Possibly *limutte*(*t*[*e*) . . .].

[3] Possibly the end of the sign 𒀹𒁹𒌅, *li*.

No. 7 [R 2, 606].[1]

TRANSLITERATION.

1. [*ᵐ ⁱˡᵘŠulmânu*](*nu*)-*ašaridu*
2. [*ša-ak-nu ⁱˡᵘBêl šangû ⁱˡᵘ*]*Aššur šarru dan-nu*[1]
3. [. . . . . *ša*]-*ap-ra-ti pa-ki-id*
4. [. . . . . *e*]*tillûti ka-ši-id mul-tar-ḫi*
5. [. . . . . . *a*]-*na ši-id-di na-as-ku-ti ˢᵃᵇᵘKu-tɪ-ɪ*
6. [. . . . *Lu-u*]*l-lu-mi-i u Šu-ba-ri-i da-iš mâtâti ia-bɪ*
7. [. *apil ᵐPu*]-*di-ilu ša-ak-ni ⁱˡᵘBêl šangû Aššur-ma e-mu-ma*
8. [. . . . . . . ,]-*bi e-na-ḫu-ma iḫ-tab-tu si-kur-ra-te*
9. [. . . . ⁱˡᵘIšta*]*r bêlti-ia an-šu-su-nu u-ni-kir ma-ak-te*
10. [. . . . . .]*e-pu-uš na-ri-ia u ti-me-ni-ia aš-ku-un*
11. [. . . . . .]*i-še-me mu-ni-kir ši-iṭ-ri-ia u šu-mi-i*[*a*]
12. [. . .]*mât-su li-ib-ri-iḳ a-na mâti-šu ḫu-ša-ḫi l*[*id-di*]

TRANSLATION.

1. [Shalma]neser,
2. [the governor of Bel, the priest of] Ashur, the mighty king,
3. [. . . . of] tributary gifts, who careth for
4. [. . . of] dominion, who had conquered the mighty,
5. [. . . un]to the lordly districts of the Ḳutî
6. [. . . . the Lu]llumî and the Shubarî, who hath trodden down the lands of the foe,
7. [. . . . the son of Pu]di-ilu, the governor of Bêl, the priest of Ashur. When
8. [. . . .] fell into ruins and the enclosed spaces[2] had been rifled,[3]

---

[1] For the text, see below, p. 173. The fragment measures 5⅛ in. by 3¾ in.

[2] Prob. not for *zi-kur-ra-te*, "temple-towers."

[3] The reading *iḫ-tab-tu*, I 2 from *ḫabâtu*, with passive meaning, is more probable than *'i-tab-tu*, I 2 from *abâtu*.

9. [. . . Ishta]r, my lady, their ruined state I altered,
and that which was fallen

10. [. . . .] I built, and my memorial tablets and my
cylinders I set in place.

11. [. . . . . and Ishtar unto his prayer] shall
hearken. But whosoever shall alter my inscription
or my name (which is thereon)

12. [. . . .] his land may [Adad] blast, and upon his
land may he cast famine !

Two more fragments of bowl inscriptions are published
in this appendix as Nos. 8 and 9, the former because
it may with considerable probability be assigned to
Tukulti-Ninib I, and the latter as it gives another
instance of the use of the form *mu-ni-kir* during the
early Assyrian period for the Part. II 1 of *nakâru*.[1]
The text of 56-9-9, 162, the fragment which may
probably be assigned to Tukulti-Ninib I, is transliterated
and translated below :—

No. 8 [56-9-9, 162].[2]

TRANSLITERATION.

[. . . .]
1. [. . . . . . *ḫ*]*ur-ša-ni-šu-*[*nu* . . . . . .]
2. [. . . . . .] *mâtu Pu-uš-še* [. . . . . .]

---

[1] The fragment No. 9 (K. 14921) gives only a few words ; its text
reads : 1. [. . . . .] 2. *u-tir* [. . . . .] 3. *a-bi-ia a-na* [. . . . .]
4. *mu-ni-kir ši-*[*iṭ-ri-ia* . . . . .] 5. *ša-a-šu mât-s*[*u* . . . . .]. The fragment is evidently inscribed with parts of the concluding lines of a building
inscription.

[2] For the text, see below, p. 175. The fragment measures 3¼ in. by
2⅝ in.

3. [. . . . . .]-*me-ri-šu-nu a*-[. . . . . .]
4. [. . . . .]-*lu-ma mi-iṣ-ri-ti-ša*[. . . . .]
5. [. . . .] *arbâ*(*a*) *šarrâni*^{pl} *mâtâti N*[*a-'i-ri* . .]
6. [. . . . .]

TRANSLATION.

[. . . . .]
1. [. . . . . .] their highlands [· . . . .]
2. [. . . . . .] the land of Pushshe [. . . .]
3. [. . . . . . .] their [. . . . . . .]
4. [. . . . . .] the boundaries thereof [. . .]
5. [. . . . .] forty kings of the lands of N[a'iri .]
6. [. . . . .]
[. . . . .]

It will be seen that the fragment is inscribed with a
summary of conquests, which include "highlands"
in l. 1, "the land of Pushshe" in line 2, and "forty
kings of the lands of N[a'iri]" in l. 5. A comparison of
these phrases with the account of the conquests of
Tukulti-Ninib I in the Annals, ll. 12, 14, and 21 (see
above pp. 80 ff.) would seem to show that the bowl,
of which 56–9–9, 162 is a fragment, was inscribed with
a text of Tukulti-Ninib I. From his brick-inscriptions
found at Kuyunjik we know that Tukulti-Ninib I
restored the temple of Ishtar at Nineveh, and we may
assume that this bowl, and possibly the fragment No. 6,
were inscribed to commemorate the same event. As in
the bowl-inscriptions of his father, Shalmaneser I, the
account of his building operations was preceded by a
list of his conquests and his genealogy.

CUNEIFORM TEXTS.

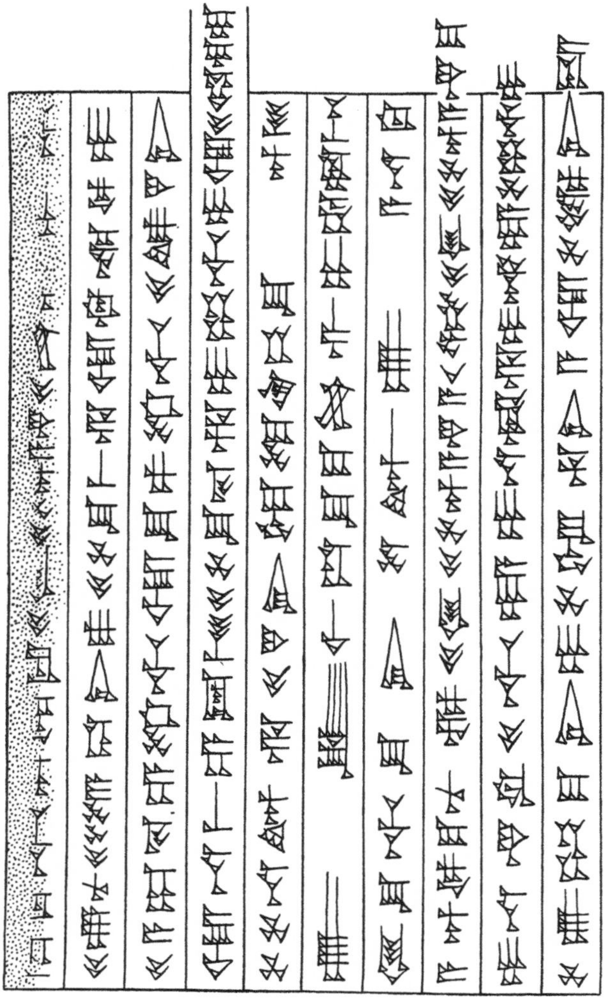

The Annals of Tukulti-Ninib I, Obverse, ll. 1–10.

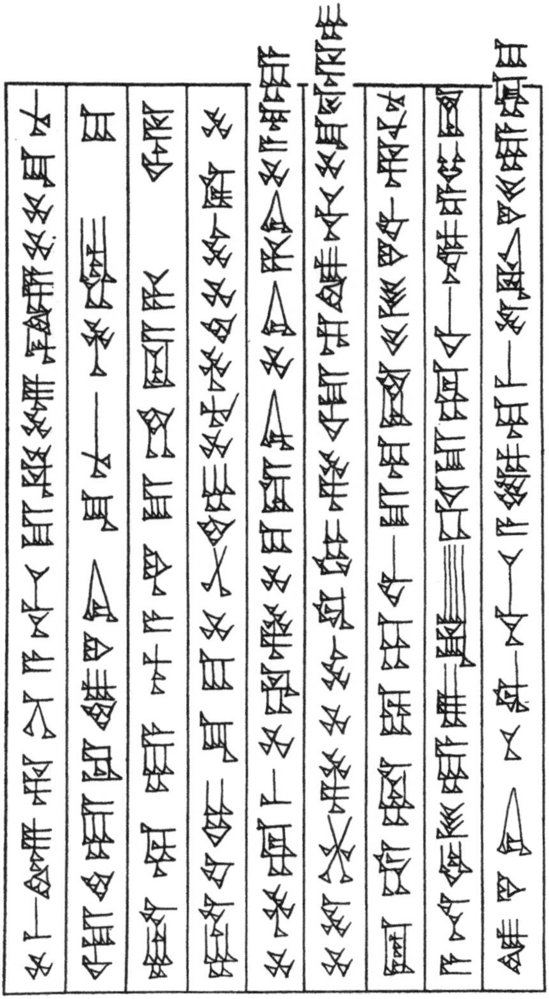

The Annals of Tukulti-Ninib I, Obverse, ll. 11–19.

The Annals of Tukulti-Ninib I, Obverse, ll. 20–28.

20

25

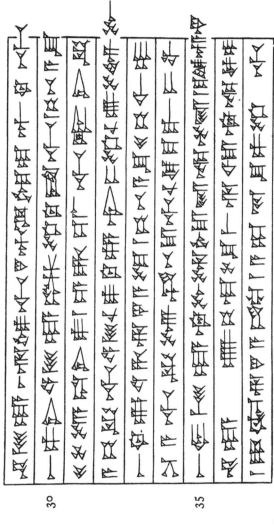

The Annals of Tukulti-Ninib I, Obverse, ll. 29–37.

30

35

The Annals of Tukulti-Ninib I, Reverse, ll. 1-9.

The Annals of Tukulti-Ninib I, Reverse, ll. 10-17.

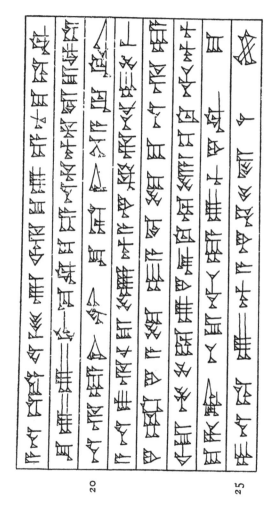

The Annals of Tukulti-Ninib I, Reverse, ll. 18-25.

30

The Annals of Tukulti-Ninib I, Reverse, ll. 26–30.

Portion of the Babylonian Chronicle, 82–7–4,38, referring to the reign or Tukulti-Ninib I [Col. IV, ll. 1–13].

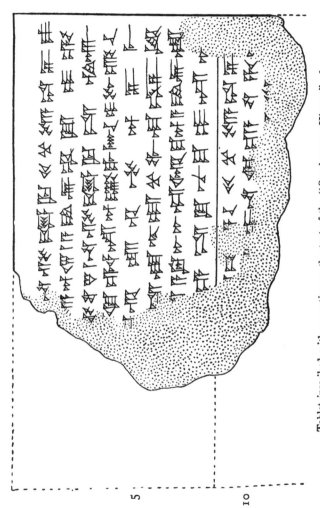

Tablet inscribed with a portion of the text of the "Synchronous History" of
Babylonia and Assyria [S. 2106, Obverse].

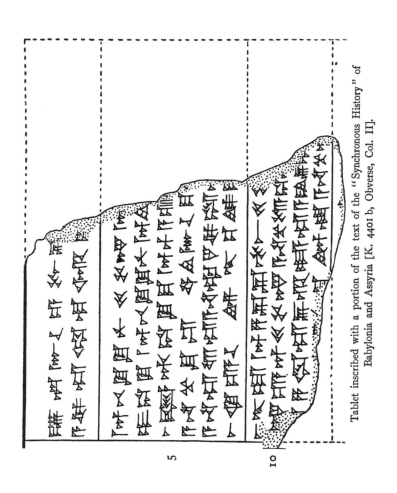

Tablet inscribed with a portion of the text of the "Synchronous History" of Babylonia and Assyria [K. 4401 b, Obverse, Col. II].

m

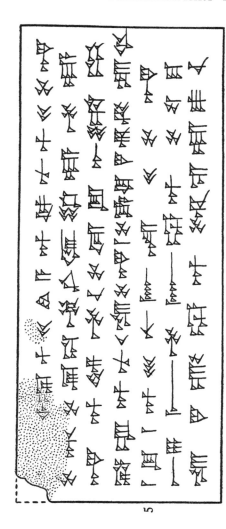

OBVERSE.

EDGE.

Seal-inscriptions of Shagarakti-Shuriash and Tukulti-Ninib I, from a tablet of the time of Sennacherib [K. 2673].

REVERSE.

Seal-inscriptions of Shagarakti-Shuriash and Tukulti-Ninib I, from a tablet of the time of
Sennacherib [K. 2673].

No. 1. [56-9-9, 164.]

No. 2. [56-9-9, 181.]

No. 3. [56-9-9, 187.]

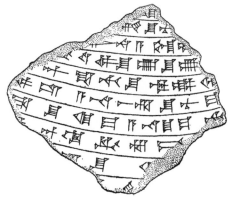

No. 4. [S. 2115.]

No. 5. [S. 2125].

No. 6.

[56-9-9, 180.]

No. 7.

[R. 2, 606.]

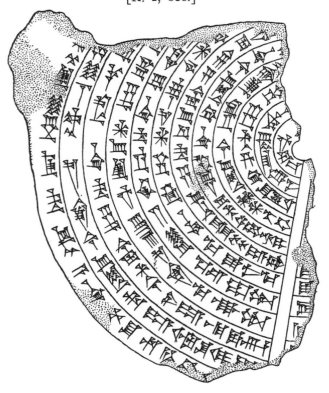

No. 8.
[56–9–9, 162.]

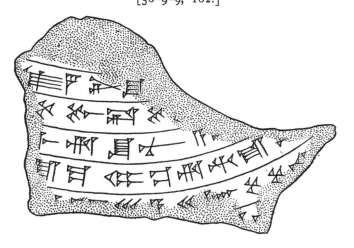

No. 9.
[K. 14921.]

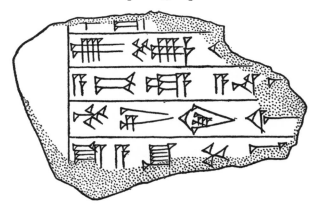

INDEX.

ABÛ-HABBA, temple of the Sun-god at, 32.

ABYDOS, foundation deposits from, 21, 25 f. ; position of foundation deposits at, 38 ; foundation pits at, 38.

ADAD, his temple built in Kar-Tukulti-Ninib, 40, 88 f. ; his statue carried to Babylon, 64, 116 ff. ; his statue recovered by Sennacherib, 64; invoked by Shalmaneser I, 131 f., 136; invoked by Tukulti-Ninib I, 106 f., 108 f., 134.

ADAD-NIRARI I, description of his memorial tablet, 2 ; his tablet compared with that of Tukulti-Ninib I, 3 f. ; record of his conquests, 2 ; subdued the Ḳutî, 46 ; defeated Nazi-marattash, 59, 100 f. ; restored the temple of Ashur, 2 ; in the genealogy of Shalmaneser I, 126 f., 130 f. ; in the genealogy of Tukulti-Ninib I, 80 f., 134.

ADAD-NIRARI III, his reference to Bêl-kapkapi, 56, n. 2 ; probably restored temple of Nabû and Marduk, 51, n. 1, 125.

ADAD-SHUM-IDDINA, his position in the Babylonian List of Kings, 73 ; time of his reign according to the Chronicle (82-7-4, 38), 74 ; his relations with Tukulti-Ninib I, 74 f.

ADAD-SHUM-NAṢIR, writer of letter to two Assyrian kings, 72 ; possibly to be identified with Adad-shum-uṣur, 72 f. ; reading of his name, 72 f., n. 3.

ADAD-SHUM-UṢUR, his accession, 44, 98 f. ; slew Bêl-kudur-uṣur, 104 f. ; invaded Assyria, 104 f. ; his position in the Babylonian List of Kings, 73 ; time of his reign according to the Chronicle (82-7-4, 38), 74 f. ; his relationship to Tukulti-Ninib I, 74 ; reading of his name, 72 f., n. 3.

AKARSALLU, see KAR-ISHTAR.

AKKAD, its subjugation by Tukulti-Ninib I, 4, 13, 44, 49 f., 86 f. ; revolt of its nobles against Tukulti-Ninib I, 44, 98 f. ; seal of Tukulti-Ninib I carried from, 106 f. ; in the titles of Tukulti-Ninib I, 45, 78 f. ; in the title of Marduk-nadin-akhê, 118 f.

ALAIA, conquered by Tukulti-Ninib I, 48, 82 f. ; its position, 48.

ALZI, conquered by Tukulti-Ninib I, 48, 82 f. ; subdued by Tiglath-pileser I, 48 ; associated with Shubarî, 48 ; its position, 48.

AMASIS II, his foundation deposits from Tell Nebesha, 21 ; position of his foundation deposits, 34.

AMEN-HETEP II, foundation pits in his temple at Thebes, 37.

by Tukulti-Ninib I, 13, 43, 82 f. ;
in title of Tukulti-Ninib I, 45,
78 f. ; associated with Alzi and
Purukuzzu, 48 ; its importance,
48 ; its position, 48.

SHUZIGASH, usurped the throne of
Kadashman-kharbe (according to
the Chronicle 82–7–4, 38), 59,
n, 1.

SHUZUBU, carried to Assyria by
Sennacherib, 116 f.

SIN-IDINNAM, governor of Larsam,
54.

SIPPAR, temple of the Sun-god at,
32.

SULILI, early Assyrian king, 56,
n. 2.

SUMER, its subjugation by Tukulti-
Ninib I, 4, 13, 44, 49 f., 86 f. ;
in title of Tukulti-Ninib I, 45,
78 f.

SUMERIANS, time of their predomi-
nance in Babylonia, 53.

SUN-GOD, his temple at Sippar,
32 f.

SUN-GOD TABLET, of Nabû-pal-
iddina, 31 ff.

SUSA, 54.

SYNCHRONOUS HISTORY, its value
for early history of Assyria, 1 ;
discrepancies between it and the
Chron. 82–7–4, 38, 59, n. 1, 75 ;
translation of passage from,
100 ff. ; cited, 8, 50, n. 1, 58 f.

SYRIA, Northern, 48.

TA-USERT, foundation deposits from
her temple at Thebes, 25 ; position of her foundation deposits,
37.

TEARZI, conquered by Tukulti-
Ninib I, 48, 82 f. ; its position,
48.

TELL GEMAYEMI, see GEMAYEMI.

TELL DAFNA, see DAFNA.

TELL EL-AMARNA, 57, n. 4.

TELL LOH, bronze statues of Gudea
from, 33, n. 1.

TELL NEBESHA, see NEBESHA.

THEBES, foundation deposits from,
25 ; position of foundation deposits
at, 37 ; foundation pits at, 37.

THOTHMES III, received gifts from
Assyrian kings, 57 ; his foundation
deposits from Abydos, 21 ; foundation deposit of his at Nubt, 27,
n. 1 ; foundation pits in his small
temple at El-Kâb, 37.

TIGLATH-PILESER I, conquered
Mekhri, 46 ; conquered Kumanî,
46 f. ; defeated the forces of Kummukhi and the Kurtê, 48 ; subdued Alzi and Purukuzzu, 48 ;
conquered Na'iri, 49 ; statues of
Adad and Shala carried to Babylon
in his time, 64, 118 f. ; his references to building operations of
early Assyrian kings, 1 ; his
reference to Ishme-Dagan and
Shamshi-Adad, 55 ; obscure
similes in his Cylinder-inscription,
86 f., n. 1 ; his Cylinder-inscription cited, 4 ; inscriptions of his
wrongly assigned to Shalmaneser
I, 124 f.

TIGRIS, 102 f.

TÛKH EL-KARAMÛS, foundation
deposits from, 20 f., n. 2 ;
remains of foundation sacrifice at,
25.

TUKULTI-ASHUR, possibly succeeded Ashur-naṣir-pal I, 72 ;
restoration of Marduk's statue to
Babylon in his time, 100 f. ;
Tukulti-Ninib's seal possibly
restored to Babylon in his time,
63, n. 2 ; correct reading of his
name, 72, n. 1.

TUKULTI-NINIB I, his reign an
epoch in Assyrian and Babylonian
history, 50 ; his campaigns, 43 ff.,
80. ff. ; defeated and deported
Bibeashu to Assyria, 50, 86 f. ;
recent views as to his date with
reference to that of Bibeashu, 7 f. ;
his conquest of Babylon, 4, 96 ff. ;

For EU product safety concerns, contact us at Calle de José Abascal, 56–1°,
28003 Madrid, Spain or eugpsr@cambridge.org.